To Mary!
Keep it up!

Nancy Robinson Masters

A confident, slender girl with laughing eyes

ALL MY DOWNS HAVE BEEN UPS

All My Downs

Have Been Ups

Nancy Robinson Masters

ISBN 0-9623563-2-8

Production:	John R. Matthews, Inc.
Cover design:	Debra Warr
Copy editor:	Robin Saylor
Cover photo:	Ken Ellsworth

MasAir Publications
Abilene, Texas

Acknowledgements

I am indebted to innumerable writers, editors, publishers, friends and other sources who have provided material for my stories.

I am especially indebted to Oleta Dockrey Rogers Whitt, without whom there would have been no "Ups and Downs" newspaper column, and no Nancy Robinson Masters.

My sister, Gale Robinson Hargrove, and my brother, Jerry Paul Robinson, have shared all of my downs and ups with patience, understanding and love that goes beyond anything I deserve.

The only way I can express my appreciation to them for being the very best big sister and big brother in the whole world is to remind them of how blessed they are that I wasn't twins.

Some I wrote for money,
Some I wrote for fun.
Some I wrote and threw away
And never sang to anyone.
One I wrote for Mama,
And a couple still aren't through
I've lost track of all the rest—
But the most I wrote for you.

—The Statler Brothers
"Some I Wrote"
©Polygram Records by permission

Flight Plan

Foreword

"Come fly with me," Nancy Robinson Masters invites.

Readers who have taken Nancy up on this invitation for the past fifteen years aren't the only ones who are in for a thrill when they read and re-read her favorite stories selected from the more than 3,000 that have been published in magazines, newspapers, trade journals and corporate communications around the world.

Those who are "flying" with Nancy for the first time will wonder why it has taken so long for them to be introduced to this Texas writer who weaves wind, wings and words into stories you will think she wrote just for you.

These are stories peopled with real characters: Dr. John Brinkley of goat gland fame; Antarctic explorer Robert Falcon Scott; crop-duster cowboys and rain-making Indians; voodoo queens and today's civilian and military adventurers who ride herd over the skies.

There are also those characters who may not be real in the truest sense of fact. They are the ones whose names Nancy admits to having changed in order to protect *her* innocence. But they are real to Nancy. And she makes them real to us.

Nancy takes us to places we never heard of and places we pass by every day. She lets us put our feet on the rudders and our hand on the throttle. She makes us fly the airplane when it would be easier to stay on the ground.

Collections of an author's favorite works are too often one-dimensional. What you will discover here is the exception. This is a deeper look "under the cowling" at the stories behind the stories and the writer behind the words. It isn't always a smooth ride, but the landings are safe every time.

Robert Flynn

The Robinson kids: Jerry Paul, Gale and Nancy

Preflight

Some portions of this book are absolute fact.
Some are absolute fiction.

All that matters is how you choose to see it.

If I tell you which is which, you won't
have the pleasure of deciding for yourself.

I want you to have the pleasure.

Some portions of me are absolute fact.
Some are absolute fiction.

All that matters is how you choose to see me.

If I tell you which is which, you won't
have the pleasure of deciding for yourself.

I want you to have all of the pleasure.

And some of the pain.

η R M

Lost in barnstormer wonderland

1

Bradley T. Goes Flying

Even a child is known by his doings. —Proverbs 20:11

It was the postman who first knew something was wrong at the Robinson house that miserably hot afternoon in June.

Usually the stereo was blaring Willie Nelson through the open windows of the living room when he made his delivery rounds. That Saturday, however, the living room windows were closed and the blinds drawn shut as if the sagging old house did not want to know summer had come to West Texas again.

A paper sack of fresh-picked black-eyed peas waiting to be snapped shriveled in the sun on the back porch.

The petunias in the singed washtub needed watering.

Cuptowels fluttered dryly on the clothes line in the back lot.

The only sounds the postman heard were the screeching of the mulberry limbs scratching the woodpile where Bradley T.'s rickety sawhorse rotted...

And the dull thud of the newspaper as it landed on yesterday's mail still in the box.

The postman knew something was wrong. But he did not know LaDelle Robinson was dead.

15

Most of the folks in Jones County could remember the time LaDelle Robinson canceled her subscription to the weekly hometown newspaper.

She told editor Roy Craig it was because the paper was becoming "pornographic."

It began with an advertisement (complete with graphic drawings) for the new "inflation" bras that had just arrived at one of the local dry goods stores.

LaDelle was horrified.

A couple of weeks later a movie advertisement for *Niagara*, starring Marilyn Monroe and Joseph Cotton, appeared in the Grand Theater listings. The ad touted the movie as "The story of a wayward wife whose desires were as endless as the swirling rapids of Niagara."

Well, that did it.

Pornography might come to Stamford, LaDelle politely informed Craig. But it would not come to her mailbox. She was canceling her subscription until he repented. Furthermore, she added sternly, she would pray for the Grand Theater to go out of business.

Whether Roy Craig ever repented or not is unknown.

But a few years later the Grand Theater flashed its final flick and closed its doors.

Most of the locals credited the arrival of television for the Grand's demise, but I had a pretty good idea it was more on account of LaDelle Robinson. I knew first hand how powerful her praying could be...

She was my mother.

Bradley T. wasn't normal.

Of course "normal" didn't really mean much to the kids on the east side of town where Highway 6 came through. To us he was just one more jelly bread sandwich to fix when we ate under the mulberry trees. That he couldn't talk and didn't go to school even though he was the same age as my big brother didn't concern us because Mama had taught us Bradley T. was "special."

Mama knew why he was special but she never told us. What we did know was that the surest way to get your legs switched redder than a July sunburn was to treat Bradley T. as if he wasn't as good as we were.

"Would you like to have grape jelly on your bread, Bradley T.?" Mama would ask when we all lined up on the back step for lunch.

She asked him that same question every day even though she knew he couldn't say "yes ma'am" like the rest of us were expected to do.

The best part of eating jelly sandwiches was seeing who could lick their bread the quickest. Or guessing how many ants it took to haul a glob of the sweet stuff away if some accidentally dropped on the grass.

Bradley T. licked slower than anybody, but he never, ever dropped any jelly.

Never.

Sometimes Bradley T. made noises that Mama said were his way of talking. However, when Bradley T. *really* wanted your attention, he would give your hand a hard, hard squeeze.

Pointing was also one of his "special" ways. We didn't always understand what he was pointing at or why. Mama said it wasn't important for us to know.

"In his own mind Bradley T. can do anything you can do," she said. "That's all that matters, and don't you ever forget it."

We took turns making sure somebody was always looking out for Bradley T. Mama made a rule that whoever got to pick first when we were choosing sides for baseball or Red Rover got the privilege of having Bradley T. on their team.

It didn't matter which team got Bradley T. He would stand by whoever was pitching and point his finger toward the ragged chair cushion we used for home plate.

We played a zillion games of baseball and Bradley T. was always on the mound.

It was my brother who came up with the idea of putting one of the ragged chair cushions over Daddy's wobbly sawhorse to make a saddle. He used a tarpaulin rope to make stirrups and one of Daddy's old belts to make a bridle. Then he showed Bradley T. how to ride.

We never had to worry about where Bradley T. was after that. For hours on end he would straddle that sawhorse, gripping the belt with one hand and pointing up with the other. With his feet hooked into the rope stirrups he was off in cowboy wonderland.

When the rest of us would get tired of playing cowboys and move on to making mud pies or stomping grasshoppers we'd try to get him to climb down and go with us.

Bradley T. just pointed and kept riding.

Bradley T.'s mother worked at the laundry down the road. She didn't seem to mind all the time he spent in our back lot. Neither did the rest of the parents whose children congregated there. If Mama got tired of being responsible for them she would tell them to go home. Everybody except Bradley T.

She let him stay all day.

Sometimes when he was sitting by himself on the sawhorse she would go stand under the tree and talk to him. She would tell him what a good job he was doing riding that pretty horse. Just like Gene Autry and Roy Rogers, she said.

No wonder Bradley T. never wanted to go home.

When his mother did call for him, he wouldn't move.

"Bradley T., you have to go home now," Mama would tell him in her slow easy voice. Then she'd squeeze his hand.

Only then would he let go of the bridle and climb down so my brother could walk him back to the laundry.

The day I started second grade the laundry burned.

Bradley T. and his mother moved to California, and the weeds took over the charred #3 washtubs they left behind. The weeds eventually took over our back lot as well. The kids growing up by Highway 6 got too big to play Red Rover.

The sawhorse finally rode off into the sunset to the scrap wood pile. Mama would occasionally look out where it used to stand under the mulberry trees and say to no one in particular, "I wonder what ever became of Bradley T.?"

It was one of those hot Dyess Air Force Base Open House afternoons when the soles of your shoes melted to the ramp if you stood in one position too long.

Bill, my flight instructor, had flown a beautiful 1939 Stearman biplane in to display. It had a fresh red paint job and wings so slick a bug couldn't stand on them. Old people and little kids alike lined up for a chance to sit in the open cockpit and imagine what it was like to be the Great American Barnstormer of days gone by.

I was returning from my third trip to get Bill a soda pop when I saw a bus from State School pulled up next to the Stearman. A crowd of neatly dressed residents were clumsily trying to climb on the wingwalk of the airplane.

"My turn, my turn," two gray-haired men were crying in childish frustration.

"Make him get out," another demanded.

"I want to fly, too," another begged.

Amid the noisy commotion of two dozen frantic, mentally challenged adults all trying to get in the airplane at once, Bill and the sponsors of the group were tugging hopelessly at the enormous person wedged inside the front cockpit.

It was Bradley T.

He was sitting with his feet locked under the rudder bars and his finger steadfastly pointing toward the instrument panel. He had grown up physically—his right hand had a grip on the wooden control stick that would have crushed steel—but his mind was forever locked in a three-year old's world.

Bradley T. was oblivious to the badgering of his peers. He was lost in barnstormer wonderland.

"Shut up," I yelled, rudely pushing my way through the crowd. "Bradley T. can't hear you when you holler."

The noise quietened. Bill looked at me as if I'd lost my mind but moved to give me room to squat on the wingwalk.

"Bradley T., you have to go home now," I whispered in his ear. Slow and easy just like Mama used to do. Then I squeezed his hand. Hard.

His expression never changed, but his hand relaxed from the control stick. I told him I was glad to see him and that he sure was doing a good job flying that pretty airplane.

Just like Gene Autry and Roy Rogers, I said.

Bradley T. smiled.

He calmly pushed himself up out of the cockpit with one hand while still pointing with the other. Bill showed him how to slide down the wingwalk to the ramp.

I walked him to the bus.

The last time I saw Bradley T. he was sitting in the seat behind the bus driver eating a jelly sandwich.

Mama was right. In his own mind Bradley T. could do anything I could do.

Even fly.

Just a little monoplane built by the Interstate Aircraft Corporation

2

The Aviatrix and The Instructor

Take fast hold of instruction; let her not go. —Proverbs 4:13

We were shelling black-eyed peas on the back porch late one Saturday evening. I was ten-wanting-to-be-eighteen.

"Mama, what's a 'wayward wife?'" I asked.

Mama never took her eyes off her lap as she squared her plump shoulders and brushed the pea hulls out of her apron.

"A woman who is married but doesn't know it," she said.

I wasn't sure I understood how a woman could be married without knowing it, but I played like I did anyway.

Then I told her I wanted one of those new inflation bras.

"You've got about as much need for one of those right now as you have for an airplane," she said, sternly pursing her lips to keep from laughing.

I was stunned.

How on earth did Mama know I wanted an airplane? I had not told a soul that I had been watching the duster pilots from our turnrow and had decided if I could fly an airplane I could go somewhere—anywhere—just as long as it was so far away I never had to worry again about too much drought or too little money.

When I told her my plan she slowly shook her head and sighed.

"Flying won't take you away from trouble. Trouble will be sitting behind you every time you take off and waiting for you every time you land."

Mama didn't know how right she was.

———————

She was just a little monoplane built by the Interstate Aircraft Corporation. Her wings were structured with solid spruce spars. Her fuselage of welded tubular steel was covered with Grade A cotton fabric from cabin to tailwheel, and her one oleospring shock-absorbing unit served both legs of the landing gear.

Her days were spent giving simple pleasure to those who mounted her two tandem seats for a closer view of the wild, blue yonder.

Pearl Harbor changed all that.

Like "Lucky Strike Green" the little Interstate Cadet went to war. At the request of the U.S. Army authorities in 1941 she left flying for pleasure behind and was developed into a light liaison and observation plane of the Grasshopper class.

Many a pilot was surprised to find her look of easy innocence deceptive. Her steerable tailwheel demanded far more skill than most cocky cadets cared to admit.

Ironically, one little Interstate Cadet survived the war only to meet disaster in the highline wires stretching across the open fields of north Texas. For nine years N37205 lay untouched in a crumpled heap in the corner of a barn. Then she was resurrected like the Phoenix to fly again.

Thirty-eight years after Pearl Harbor, daylight begins to break through the 25-degree cold. It is Saturday and most of the world is still asleep. But the sturdy Interstate, wearing new Dacron fabric, has been rolled out of her hangar. No Army Air Corp pilot grips her throttle this flight—only a female, born eight years after the Interstate carried her first wartime cargo.

Brakes set.

Throttle closed.

Contact.

With a swing of the varnished wooden prop, both airplane and Aviatrix clatter to life. Normally it would be just the two of them. But The Aviatrix has been away from tailwheels for several weeks, so being the proud new owner of the shiny red and black airplane she has asked that most dreaded of all creatures to join them for the morning's flight...

The Instructor.

The fear of The Instructor has been known to every student who ever wore goggles. But The Aviatrix has no fear—after all, hasn't she been flying airplanes alone, lo these many years?

Ah, yes.

But The Instructor is not impressed. As they trundle down the taxiway his calm but chilling voice calls sharply into her left ear.

"Why are you holding the stick back?"

The stick is abruptly shoved forward.

"Let's not forget that the stick goes *forward* when we taxi downwind," he reminds her with wicked satisfaction.

While The Instructor sits back with arms folded and eyes partially closed, The Aviatrix opens the throttle and with 65 thundering horsepower the Interstate rumbles down the runway leaving behind a flurry of tailwheel dust.

"Next time try keeping *both* wheels on the pavement," he sneers.

The Instructor *knows* how The Aviatrix hates it when he sneers.

"Don't hold rudder in the turn!"

He doesn't even have his eyes open. How could he possibly know the ball is not centered?

"You're flying right wing low—wings level, *please*."

The Instructor is even more unbearable when he is polite.

"You keep climbing when you're supposed to be at altitude. Why don't you just *trim* the airplane?"

The Aviatrix begins to wonder at the wisdom of having The Instructor along. This was supposed to have been a *pleasant* flight.

"You'd better reduce power before the engine blows up."

The only thing about to blow up is The Aviatrix.

"Your base leg is too close to the runway.

"You're not making your crosswind corrections.

"Remember when you flare to keep the stick all the way back and use your feet to stay on the runway."

The Aviatrix would love to pull the stick back—all the way down his throat.

With a thud they turn off the runway and roll to a stop. For some strange reason The Aviatrix feels weak. Her sweaty palms on a freezing morning are a dead giveaway that The Instructor succeeded. She avoids looking at his scowling face as he climbs out the door.

"You're alright, kid. You don't need me anymore." He ducks to miss the wing and shuffles away.

Ah! Perhaps it is a good thing that Instructors and Interstates haven't changed all that much since Pearl Harbor.

They both know how to keep an Aviatrix humble.

Signature du Titulaire

Bessie Coleman

The first black woman in the world to have earned an International
Pilot's License.   Courtesy Institute of Texan Cultures

3

Brave Bessie

Women should empty the slops and attend to the domestic affairs for which nature intended them. By taking this advice they will gain the respect of all right minded people—an end not to be attained by meddling in masculine concerns of which they are profoundly ignorant. —Henry Wright, anti-women's-suffrage leader

---

I was born on a howling February morning in the basement of the hospital.

Usually only black people were admitted to the basement. Just before midnight, however, the hospital boiler quit. There wasn't any heat on the second floor where the white babies were always delivered—too much rust from the red mud water of the Brazos River had finally done the old boiler in—so Nurse Lavelle quickly moved everything, including Mama and the nurses' station Motorola radio to the only warm place left in the hospital.

Dr. Metz came whistling in declaring it never failed for a baby to come at the worst possible time. The announcer giving the 4 a.m. weather report said the temperature outside was 12 degrees with a blowing West Texas snow storm.

The announcer also noted February 4th marked the birthday of the famous "Lone Eagle" aviator, Charles Lindbergh.

None of the people in the hospital basement heard his report, however, due to the lusty yells of the new Robinson baby girl.

"Damn beautiful baby," Dr. Metz said. It was what he always said about every baby he delivered.

There was another "damn beautiful" baby girl born later that day in the hospital basement though I didn't meet her until we were in the seventh grade.

That was the first year black children were allowed to attend our school.

What Mama lacked in physical stature she made up for by being plain spoken.

One night some people came out to our place to get Mama to sign a petition warning black children not to come to our school.

She told them since none of the black women said a word against her having a baby in their basement, she wasn't about to say a word against a black child getting an education in our school.

The best thing they could do, Mama advised, was take their petition and move on.

They moved.

She was brilliant.

She was beautiful.

She was black.

Before Women's Lib in the '70s, the Equal Opportunity Act of the '60s and even before the Civilian Pilot Training Program (CPTP) of 1939, which stated that no one could be denied pilot training on account of "race, creed or color," Miss Bessie Coleman had determined, dared and done the impossible.

She had become the first American licensed female black pilot.

While the history of blacks in the United States is fraught with appalling prejudice and injustice, it was in the world of aviation that black men and women were first able to overcome the "color line" barriers and be accepted for their abilities rather than their race.

It wasn't easy.

Bessie was born January 20, 1896, in Atlanta, Texas. Her mother was Negro. Her father one-fourth Negro, three-fourths Indian.

"We picked cotton in Texas, and I'd look up and think, 'If I'm ever going to have a better life I've got to get above these fields,'" she once told a newspaper editor.

"I read everything I could get my hands on about airplanes. Some of the libraries wouldn't let black girls who picked cotton borrow books. But the books I wanted were about piloting, and it surprised folks so much they let me read them anyway."

Bessie left Texas for Oklahoma, then on to Chicago where she put herself through beauty school to become a manicurist. She worked in a chili parlor, saving for months to have enough money to take flying lessons.

It wasn't only lack of funds that kept Bessie from her childhood dream. No one in the United States in 1921 would teach a black woman how to fly.

On the advice of a newspaper publisher in Chicago named Robert Abbott, Bessie began taking French lessons. Once she had mastered the language she took her savings and went to Europe to learn to fly at Anthony Fokker's School of Aviation.

In 1922 Bessie Coleman returned to Chicago, the first black woman in the world to have earned an International Pilot's License.

"I knew if I could get black people to see how my determination had paid off, they would be inspired not only to learn to fly but to pursue whatever they wanted to do in spite of the obstacles of society."

It worked. At her first air show exhibition given at what is now Chicago's Midway Airport, more than 3,000 spectators jammed the gates to see her aerobatic performance.

It was the same in Houston, Wharton and Wichita Falls. Almost before Bessie had completed her routine of figure eights and dives, with landings so perfect she lifted not a trace of dust, Negro flying clubs were being organized across the country.

In Austin, Bessie was entertained by "Ma" Ferguson, then Governor of Texas. She told Ferguson, "I am right on the threshold of opening a school. A school where blacks can learn to fly or to work on airplanes and when they have shown they can do this they will have the courage to quit riding the back of trains."

Bessie Coleman did not live to see her new dream fulfilled. On April 30, 1926, while performing an exhibition in Florida, she was catapulted from her open cockpit biplane during an abrupt nose dive. (The airplane was not equipped with seatbelts.)

A mechanic's wrench was later discovered wedged in the airplane's controls. Some speculated the wrench might have been deliberately left in an effort to put an end to the growing momentum Bessie Coleman's aviation accomplishments had triggered.

If such speculations were true, the sabotage was a complete failure.

Shortly after her death William J. Powell began organizing Bessie Coleman Aero Groups to promote continued air-mindedness in the black community. "Remember Brave Bessie" became the civil rights theme song.

On Labor Day, 1931, the flying clubs sponsored the first all-black airshow in the United States, an event that attracted 15,000 spectators. From these clubs evolved such well known groups as the Tuskegee Airmen, the 99th Fighter Squadron, the integrated military services and most recently the Organization of Black Airline Pilots.

William Powell later wrote, "Because of Bessie Coleman we have overcome that which is much worse than racial barriers. We have overcome the barriers within ourselves to dare to dream."

In his book *Watching My Race Go By* Ross D. Brown said, "She fought and flew ahead of her time. She was greatly misunderstood. The things she worked for have brought honors for others to claim."

To those who sought a federal holiday in honor of a great civil rights leader: Why did you forget Bessie Coleman?

4

Easter Story

. . . be ready always to give an answer to every man that asketh you a reason of the hope that is in you. —I Peter 3:15

The abandoned hospital building was razed several years ago. They pushed the last pile of rubble into the corner of the basement where for more than three decades Big Johnny, the janitor, made plaster for all the casts that healed our town's broken bones.

When he wasn't mopping floors or mixing plaster, Big Johnny made little kids who were hurting laugh with his stories and songs. Little kids like me, whose appendix ruptured the Easter Sunday morning after my third birthday.

While Mama prayed and Daddy paced, Big Johnny carried me to the operating room singing "Old McDonald Had a Farm."

Dr. Metz told Mama I was sound asleep before they ever started the anesthetic. Good thing, too. Another minute and instead of the putrid poison filling his gloved surgeon's hand, it would have filled me.

Now there is a fine, new hospital on the east side of town with a computer-controlled heating system and a television in every room.

I don't know who makes the casts anymore, but I am sure it isn't the janitor.

Ee-ay-ee-ay-oh.

We were eastbound, climbing into the sun that greets the first flight of American Eagle Airlines each weekday morning as it departs Abilene Regional Airport.

Mornings are my favorite times to ride the Eagle. Coffee is always extra fresh, wind is zero and the airplane seems to enjoy getting off the ground like a thoroughbred being turned out of the gate for the first run of the day.

There's not too much talky-talk among the passengers, either. Most read the paper or catch a few more winks of sleep before arriving in Dallas where they will connect with flights traveling to Chicago, New York, Los Angeles, Jeddah. . .

Jeddah? Was that anywhere near New Orleans, I asked the young man sitting next to me? We had exchanged sections of the newspaper, and I had asked him where he was headed. It's one of those things I always do when I travel on the airlines because it usually leads to a story.

He laughed, accompanying his laugh with a negative shake of his head.

"Jeddah is near Mecca, Saudi Arabia. I am going home for a pilgrimage."

"Will you be home in time for Easter?" I quizzed, savoring the hot coffee I'd just had refilled.

"Easter? Easter is for Christians. I am not a Christian; I am a servant of Muhammad. Those who wish to celebrate Easter go to Jerusalem where thousands of Christians go each year at this time."

He laughed and shook his head again.

"It's hard to believe," he said.

"There really is nothing for them to see in Jerusalem but an empty tomb."

He asked if I'd ever been to Saudi Arabia.

"No, uh, but, um. . . well, I'd like to go to Jerusalem."

Then hastily I added, "I'm a Christian."

He shrugged and looked away as if to ignore further conversation.

"How far is it from Jeddah to Jerusalem?" I asked meekly, hoping he would give me a chance to explain why I thought being a Christian going to Jerusalem was better than being a follower of Muhammad going to Jeddah.

He politely said he did not know and resumed reading his paper. We both lapsed into silence again. It is 50 minutes from Abilene to Dallas on the Eagle, but those last 10 seemed like hours. How, I wondered, did this handsome young Moslem end up in Abilene? A university student? An oil shiek's son?

I ventured to ask.

"Abilene is, as you Christians would say, my mission field. I am Muhammad's servant." He was obviously pleased to tell me again.

The pilot reduced power and we began a slow descent into Dallas/Fort Worth Airport.

"Did you know Jeddah's International Airport can handle 80,000 pilgrims at any time traveling to Mecca?"

It was his turn to make polite conversation. This time I looked away. I wanted to answer with some profound testimony. Just some simple statement that would explain the ultimate difference for those who choose the Christian way. But the words weren't there.

It was so easy to be sure of the reason for your faith in Sunday school teaching second graders; it was so hard in Seat 4A beside a true servant of Muhammad.

Too late.

We parted ways inside the D/FW terminal. With a lump in my throat that felt the size of an airplane engine, I watched him disappear in the crowd. All those years of Sunday school, Lord, and like Peter before the fire I had botched my opportunity to be a Christian witness. Why had I not been able to say something meaningful, something simple? Just one sentence that might have made a difference.

I would return to Abilene in a few hours. The servant of Muhammad still had more than 7,000 miles to go to reach Jeddah.

If you wish to celebrate Easter you should go to Jerusalem. . . there's nothing there but an empty tomb.

Hey!
Wait!
Come back!
That was it! The thing I wanted to say to him that would best explain my Christian faith was exactly what he had said to me!

There's nothing there but an empty tomb.

As we zipped back across West Texas that afternoon I imagined what an aerial view of Jerusalem must have looked like that first Easter morning in A.D. 30: Golgotha wrecked by an earthquake; the Sanhedrin Court confused and silent; the tomb of Joseph of Arimathea—empty!

The stone rolled away—not to let Jesus out, but to let all of us in! A gaping, glorious testimony to the victory of Easter.

By air it is 755 miles between Jeddah and Jerusalem.

By faith it is the difference of eternity.

The servant of Muhammad said it best:

"If you wish to celebrate Easter go to Jerusalem. There's nothing there but an empty tomb."

Hallelujah!

Belle Plaine College...once boasted a promising future.

The Exchange

I traded Today for an Hour
Spent with you, in a pasture, alone;
Except for mesquite winds and fence posts
And far away locusts' soft drone.

You took the Hour that I gave you,
And for it you gave me a day
Full of sunshine and laughter and music—
Windsongs you taught me to play.

Thief Time! You have cut to the marrow
As a knife by the surgeon's deft skill.
I closed my eyes and Today was gone,
But the Hour is with me still.

I traded Today for an Hour...
The mesquite winds will all blow away.
But I shall not regret come Tomorrow
The price that I paid for Today.

5

Paying the Fiddler

As fade the leaf and morning flower
So fade our lives each passing hour,
As dews that melt before the Sun,
So pass our lives, one by one.

Welcome to Belle Plaine, Texas.

It is said that on nights of the full moon, the grass- and cactus-covered streets once carefully plotted, curbed and properly identified by such dignified names as "Antelope" and "Redbud" are alive with the ghosts of dancers. Ladies wear pink crinoline dresses and men dressed as befitted their occupation a hundred years ago either as cowboy, businessman or craftsman appear, then disappear in the misty shadows.

Even the most hardened skeptic has been known to admit hearing faint music drifting eerily from the crumbling ruins of magnificent old Belle Plaine College—a decaying, three-storied limestone edifice now grown full of mesquite and hackberry trees within what is left of its skeletal walls.

Belle Plaine College, like the town for which it was named, once boasted a promising future. At one time during its brief decade as an institution of higher learning it had more than 300

41

students enrolled who came to study Latin, Greek, music and military science. Advertisements enticed parents to send their children to this Methodist-sanctioned school built in 1884 where "thorough courses, experienced teachers" and "mild, but firm discipline" were touted.

A symphony orchestra and as many as 15 grand pianos made its claim as the "largest music conservatory in the Southwest" unchallengeable.

But a century has passed since this once prosperous town was built on barely tamed frontier wrestled from the ravages of wind, sun and the Comanches. Now where once its main street was dominated by three saloons, a hotel and a general store, cattle graze idly and rattlesnakes slither through the rubble of rocks that remain.

Belle Plaine today is only an apparition of what was the original county seat of Callahan County. Located approximately seven miles south of Baird, Belle Plaine is hidden from paved highways in a forest of pasture land. The entire area is surrounded by barbed wire fence and is private property.

Belle Plaine will never be a "tourist trap" nor will anyone ever capitalize on its demise.

Back in 1866 Callahan County was practically untouched by the white man. In 1876 John and Clabe Merchant founded the city of Belle Plaine, supposedly naming it for the first child born on the tract, Katie Belle Magee. After the city was elected county seat in 1877 in a contest that pitted it against the equally young town of Callahan City, Belle Plaine flourished.

Adding to Belle Plaine's rapid growth were the rumors of the coming of the Texas and Pacific Railroad, "sure to be extended through the city of Belle Plaine." Eastern investors flocked to the plains of central West Texas.

As a whole the community was made up of "hard-working, moral and religious folks."

History also dutifully records the presence of the Star Saloon and the OO (Double O) Saloon. Most frontier saloons operated under the names of men, but county deed records reveal that Mrs. Sarah E. Chittum purchased Lot 6 in Block 8 in 1878 where a frame building provided space for display of spirits and standing room for customers. A black and white sign across the front informed the local residents and visitors in the town that they were approaching the "S.E. Chittum Saloon."

Students were warned that if they were seen in the saloons, they would be forbidden to ever return to Belle Plaine College.

A small but important group of artisans contributed to the growth of the frontier village. One was Thomas Russell, stone mason and contractor who patiently, with hammer and chisel, shaped the hard limestone blocks for the walls of six businesses, two residences, the county jail (which was later moved intact to Baird when the County Seat was moved) and one of the buildings for Belle Plaine College. Associated with Russell was a German immigrant by the name of Fred Gardner. Gardner's constantly in demand masonry skill was perhaps the telling factor in Belle Plaine's continual struggle to survive:

There was not enough water.

Wells produced grudgingly. Water haulers charged 25 cents a barrel for creek water that was alternately murky from excessive rain or stagnant from decaying vegetation. Hence, nearly all contracts for the erection of buildings in the business district included a clause providing for the digging, walling with stone, and plastering of an underground cistern.

Fred Gardner was estimated to have finished more than two dozen cisterns in Belle Plaine between 1878 and 1880.

Other citizens were part of the legend of Belle Plaine: Wilson Henry, a leading blacksmith, was rumored to have been so distrustful of banks that he buried all his gold somewhere in the area. The rumor appears to be just that since no gold was ever discovered.

The beauty of the women of Belle Plaine has never been disputed: Miss Peachie Jackson, Miss Kate Hill, Miss Susie Austin and Mrs. Larkin Hearn were said to rival any catalog cover girl. Newcomers arriving in the town were often startled to find women of such charm, education and fashion in surroundings more harsh than hospitable.

Larkin Hearn was a stockman with a particular interest in racing horses. On the Hearn estate he built a private race track, and although evidence of any wager money changing hands is lacking, the townspeople were well aware of Hearn's "recreation," which lured large groups of horse fanciers to his ranch.

Belle Plaine Cemetery today provides an insight into life in the town that speaks more eloquently than words on paper. Dozens of unmarked graves, noted only by protruding rocks, clearly indicate that all who passed through the town were neither rich nor famous. The first grave at Belle Plaine was opened sometime in the late 1870s and interments continue to the present. Some 200 graves are clustered on the little rise two miles south of the remains of the townsite. Most noticeable among the older gravestones are those of babies, small children and young mothers.

Such was the fate of many who came into the world in Belle Plaine during those years of blizzard, drought and disease. Surviving even during the years of Belle Plaine's prosperity was a gamble.

Two incidents in the history of Belle Plaine contributed to the decline and final abandonment of the site. The first was the loss of the county seat, which was moved to Baird when the T&P Railroad was routed there instead of through Belle Plaine. Nine years later the declining economy led to the closing of Belle Plaine College. Shortly thereafter Sarah Chittum's saloon served its last thirsty customer. Vacant and all but abandoned, the town claimed only four families in 1897 with one tiny store.

Belle Plaine became a ghost town.

To this day it is unknown what became of the fifteen grand pianos of the music conservatory. Most were carried away by those who either had claims against the property or by those who merely took them to keep them from inevitable deterioration.

Neatly walled flower beds in the front yards of homes like the one that belonged to the Floyd family are overgrown with thistles and sunflowers. Mr. Floyd was a respected surveyor whose wife did not know how to cook or sew—two talents a frontierswoman sorely needed to possess. Her youngest daughter recalled to me before her death, "When company would come, Mama would have to put out a long pole with a white cloth on it so that wherever Papa was he would know to come home and help her with the cooking.

"Papa made all of our clothes—even my sister's tea dresses when the college would have their Pink Tea Parties."

If you take County Road 295 to Belle Plaine Cemetery, then continue on County Road 293 to County Road 221, you will see all that is left of Belle Plaine. Two historical markers have been placed there, but the property is privately owned and trespassers are warned not to enter.

Should you hear the sounds of piano and violin music and catch a glimpse of ghostly dancers flitting through the trees, do not venture too close...

Old cisterns are extremely dangerous.

And anyone caught at Sarah Chittum's saloon must pay the fiddler.

Never took my hat off the whole time

6

Thanksgiving

It is a good thing to give thanks unto the Lord. —Psalms 92:1

The folks at the Texas Education Agency in Austin wanted to know if I could be there on Friday. That was the day I had planned to sort through all the stacks of stories I was working on and try to get ahead of the "Deadline Demon" who seemed to be constantly breathing down my neck.

However, if I was going to spend the summer as a writing consultant working with teachers from Amarillo to Zapata I had to be at that Austin meeting.

I put away the stories and got out the sectional chart.

My flight plan took me a scant 90 miles west of Meridian, the county seat of Bosque County. In spite of the beautiful view from the cockpit I did not want to look past my left wing toward the rich, rain-soaked fields along Childress Creek.

This land was once Patent No. 171 issued to my great-great-grandfather, Daniel Robinson, and wife, Nancy Robinson, by Governor Lubbock in 1863.

In 1835 young Dan Robinson rode into Texas from Alabama to take up the cause of Texas' independence. According to the

47

Texas State Archives he was part of the scouting party who captured the disguised Santa Ana and helped haul him into Sam Houston's custody.

After Texas became a republic, the Texas Rangers Muster Roll lists this same Private Dan Robinson as serving under Capt. G.B. Erath in 1839. For the next 30 years Dan never had to pay a poll tax, or pay taxes on his saddle horse, or do "road duty" because he served as a Texas "Minute Man."

The Minute Men companies were established by legislation passed by the Congress of the Republic in 1841. They were to be available at a moment's notice to "give protection" to the frontier.

Dan wasted no time selling his land patent for $50. He bought another 160 acres and soon sold 55 of those for $2.75 an acre. On the bottom of the page of this document where Nancy's signature was required in order for the sale to be legal, there is only an "X" with two words written in by the Bosque clerk:

"Her Mark."

Nancy Robinson could not read or write.

When I look at Texas 5,500 feet below I can hardly imagine the awful heartaches, struggles and frustrations my great-great-grandmother endured as a result of her illiteracy. She was one of hundreds of illiterate frontier women in Texas who could never comprehend the opportunities afforded an ordinary woman like me who today can read and write and fly airplanes as routinely as she made biscuits.

Old sins cast long shadows.

It is no secret that Dan used part of the money from the sale of the Bosque County property to finance his poker playing habit. Just months after Nancy made her mark on that piece of paper, the remaining Robinson land was foreclosed on by the tax collector and sold for the amount of delinquent taxes due: $1.68.

Hard times. Hard ways.

Dan and Nancy moved on to Callahan County.

Although Nancy Robinson never learned to read or write, she saw to it that all of her children did. She was determined they and their children would be spared the high price she paid for ignorance.

Yes sir.

I am glad I had to fly to Austin for a meeting with the Texas Education Agency before agreeing to spend the summer traveling across Texas working with teachers. Seeing the land beneath the shadow of my wing reminds me how vitally important it is for every student in Texas to be able to read and write in today's complex society.

If they cannot, every Texan—past, present and future—will lose.

When the TEA official asked me why I wanted to take on this project that will take me to twenty Texas cities in as many days, I told him it was because I owe it to Nancy Robinson.

I don't think he understood then what I meant.

Maybe now he will.

The cold wind stings my face and stops up my ears. That's what I get for hanging my head out the window of the Cessna 172 smoothly threading its way 500 feet above Highway 36.

In the left seat pilot Charl Agiza is busy patrolling AT&T's underground pipeline of fiber-optic cables. Today I am just a right-seat passenger, riding the route from Abilene to Brownwood watching our airplane's shadow slide across West Texas beneath our wings.

There is one word to describe this view: beautiful.

Patchwork acres of plowed ground, huge splotches of purple, gold and red trees, and the sharp smell of cedar burning somewhere to the south are enough to make you giddy.

Thanksgiving is still a week away, but there is no better time to count your blessings than when sighting the tiny Callahan

County community of Cottonwood to the right of the pipeline route.

Lord, how did it get to be more than 20 years since that day after Thanksgiving in Cottonwood when we buried Uncle Wyatt?

Uncle Wyatt Robinson grew up in Cottonwood along with a passel of brothers and sisters, including one Jim Robinson who was my granddaddy. Jim moved north to Jones County in 1916, but Wyatt stayed in Cottonwood.

Uncle Wyatt was a charmer. Tall, distinguished, mustached, with twinkling eyes, known far and wide as a poet and storyteller without equal.

Uncle Wyatt lived with Grandma and Grandpa Robinson and helped take care of them until they died contentedly in the old house at the bend in the road by the creek. By then he was considered a confirmed bachelor by Cottonwood standards.

That did not stop Uncle Wyatt.

Now free of his duties to the old folks, he began a passionate mail correspondence romance with a California nurse named Verna.

Uncle Wyatt's letters to Verna were literary masterpieces.

For a boy with a bare education, his prose describing the beauty of West Texas and the glory of Cottonwood would rival Thoreau.

"Rippling streams and grassy meadows," he would promise.

"Dew-drenched mornings and skies of blue."

Verna headed for Cottonwood, wooed by a gentle romantic who owned only a cowboy hat with a rolled brim and a small tract of dirt he considered a piece of heaven on earth.

The marriage lasted but Cottonwood didn't.

There were jobs in California and none in Cottonwood, and Verna wasn't one to sit around and listen to the rippling water. Lock, stock and cowboy hat, she loaded Uncle Wyatt up and they headed west.

There was one condition, however: When the time came, Uncle Wyatt wanted to be buried at Cottonwood.

He came back for a visit once while I was in high school. He'd grown hard of hearing so I played the piano for him with the pedal down the whole time. His favorite story, not counting the one about how Verna's exceptional nursing skills cured him of his impaction, was about getting on an airplane in Los Angeles and landing in Dallas in as little time as it once took him to drive a team to Cross Plains from Cottonwood.

"Never took my hat off the whole time," he'd tell us over and over again to convince us of his bravery in the airplane.

(Of course he had to sit with his knees under his chin to have room to keep his hat on, but that was beside the point.)

Daddy said it was just another one of Uncle Wyatt's fancy stories, but I admired him anyway. The man could weave magic with his words, and magic was in short supply for me at the time.

About a year later the kinfolks were gathering to give Uncle Wyatt his last request. We sat in the Methodist Church and heard the preacher read some of Uncle Wyatt's writing.

"A man with the gift of words," the preacher said. "Surely he has left his love of words and West Texas on some of those gathered here today."

Cottonwood Cemetery isn't hard to find from the air. Especially in the fall when the cedars are still green and everything else is changing colors. Uncle Wyatt and his hat have been resting there now for more than two decades alongside my great-grandparents and other assorted relatives.

I remember while we were standing there that bright November day 20-plus years ago an airplane went over just as the last "amen" was said. We all started laughing, thinking about Uncle Wyatt scrunched up in that airliner seat refusing to take off his cowboy hat.

I wonder if it was a pipeline patroller making the same run we are flying today?

Charl banks the 172 sharply to the right and we fly home through the Highway 36 Gap. Deer scurry at the sound of the engine. The school bus winds its way along dusty county roads. Brown hay bales like giant jelly rolls line the fences, and a farmer stretches up to wave as we pass over his gate.

Yes sir, this is beautiful country. I stop hanging out the window long enough to make notes for a story about Charl Agiza. But the first words I write aren't about her aviation skills or the importance of the pipeline.

The first words I scribble are about West Texas: *rippling streams and grassy meadows. . . dew-drenched mornings and skies of blue.*

That preacher was right.

Uncle Wyatt Robinson "left on someone" his love for words and for West Texas.

Thank you, Lord, that it was left on me.

7

The Average Man's Treatment

Then Abraham fell upon his face, and laughed. —Genesis 17:17

Every Sunday afternoon my sister, brother and I would trek through the back pasture behind our house to visit my grandmother Alpha Graham Robinson, who lived about a mile southeast of our place.

Granddad Jim died of pneumonia at 47. Anyone who dared ask "Mama Rob" why she never married again would be tersely informed:

"I'd rather be Jim Robinson's widow than any other man's wife."

Then she would spit twice in her snuff can.

Mama Rob always had some project under way that we were "allowed" to help with: Hoeing weeds, hanging bedclothes to sun, cleaning out the cellar and moving the furniture around were among her favorites.

What she enjoyed most, however, was putting in and taking out the wall between the living room and one of the bedrooms of the little white house my daddy and his sisters had scraped enough money together to buy for her when Granddad died.

Within a few weeks after the wall was out, Mama Rob would decide she might need another bedroom for company and here we would go hammering studs and sheetrock into place, tacking canvas and smearing paste on wallpaper under the supervision of my Aunt Iva, who was known as one of the best carpenters and plumbers in our part of the country.

A couple of weeks later Mama Rob would decide she needed a bigger living room, so out would go the wall again.

When we weren't putting in or tearing out partitions, or wrestling mattresses from one bed to the other, Mama Rob would get her bonnet and we would load up in Iva's big Buick (which seemed to always be in need of a new muffler) and head for the cemetery to "work" the family plot.

It was my favorite way to spend Sunday afternoon.

In spite of everyone's protest, Mama Rob insisted on having a cedar tree in each corner of the barren parcel of red dirt. The cedars provided little shade, multitudes of wasps, and grew to such amazing size you could not hoe or rake without getting entangled in the scratchy branches.

She fixed ice water to take with us in a big jar with a rusty lid, which we passed from mouth to mouth without fear of germs because, she said, "the rust on the lid kills them."

She knew it had to be so because she had heard it thirty years ago from Dr. John R. Brinkley on his radio broadcast. She had not missed a day since drinking water from a jar with a rusty lid.

The idea of using a clothes dryer instead of the sun was another thing the astute Dr. Brinkley warned listeners against.

"Sunshine is God's antiseptic," Mama Rob quoted as if it were scripture. "People who sleep in sheets dried in a machine are asking for The Devil's Due."

Out on the back porch one evening I heard her and the other old women whispering about two of my granddad's brothers who went off to New Mexico and died from The Devil's Due. I didn't understand why, since they didn't have clothes dryers back then.

"They never had a chance without Dr. Brinkley," Aunt Sissy Hudson said in a voice as tiny as she was. (According to Mama Rob, Aunt Sissy fell out of a tree when she was a little girl and the fall stunted her growth. That Aunt Sissy might have had a developmental abnormality before she ever fell out of the tree was never discussed.)

"If anyone could have cured them boys of the results of their sins, Doctor could have," my grandmother agreed.

And all the old women on the back porch spit in their snuff cans and sighed in believers' unison.

In order to put up the tent for folks to sit under when Mama Rob was laid to rest beside Granddad Jim, the undertaker had to tie one of the monstrous cedar trees back out of the way.

Just as Brother Bob Green was leading us in the closing prayer, the tie broke and the tree whammed against the back of the tent so hard the folks sitting on the back row jumped out of their folding chairs. Brother Bob hollered "Jesus!" and forgot to say "Amen."

I think it embarrassed the folks from the funeral home, but it didn't bother us. We knew it was just Mama Rob having the last word about her cedar trees.

He was either the greatest visionary of modern medical transplant surgery or the greatest sideshow charlatan of all time.

Either way, there can be no doubt he turned the eyes of America toward the benefits of aviation in a way that had never been dreamed of then nor equaled since.

His name was John R. Brinkley. Better known as simply "Doctor."

At a time when America was suffering in the bowels of the Great Depression, John R. Brinkley basked comfortably on a 16-acre estate in Del Rio, Texas, surrounded by imported swans, dancing penguins and Galapagos tortoises.

He had seven Cadillacs (each a different color for the days of the week), three Lockheed airplanes and an income estimated in the millions.

It has to be one of the most remarkable, yet least publicized stories of aviation history.

Brinkley's wealth came from nearby Brinkley Hospital located in the top two floors of the Del Rio Roswell Hotel. For the sum of $750, Dr. Brinkley and his wife, Minnie, would minister to man's oldest desire—to remain physically fit and "able to perform." A man could arrive one day "exhausted, inhibited by ignorant medical doctors and totally depressed" and within 48 hours be "revived, rejuvenated and ready to enjoy youth again."

What happened in between, according to the good doctor, was "the Average Man's Treatment," which Brinkley claimed to have "discovered and refined" in his early days of practice in Milford, Kansas. Simply put, the treatment involved removing the gonad glands of a billy goat and implanting them into a human male.

In the early days patients would bring their own goats. Later, the benevolent Brinkley provided a herd of "select quality" animals from which patients could *personally* pick.

"The choice, dear friend, is entirely up to you," the good doctor urged.

What Brinkley failed to tell the ever-eager inquirers who called to make arrangements to come to Del Rio was that he had been run out of Kansas by the Medical Society, who ruled his "eclectic college of medicine" degree to be a fraud. But not before he managed to make millions and even run for governor of the state, narrowly defeated by a few thousand votes.

What gave Brinkley popularity and prominence in Kansas were the two things he brought with him to Texas—a radio station and an airplane.

In Kansas he had discovered the magnitude of influence a single airplane landing in a wheatfield could bring. Stepping out of the Lockheed he was able to preach his goat-gland salvation as a "mission of mercy for mankind." Day after day he would swoop out of the sky and invite his followers to "step right up and help yourself to a look at this marvelous machine God intended for me to use to bring you health and happiness."

So well known did Brinkley's Kansas aviation exploits become that when he was invited to come to Del Rio to "escape the persecution of those of the medical practice who would have men suffer," the first promise made by certain members of the business community was that a fine "flying field" would be made available to Brinkley.

Lockheed, stock and billy goats, Brinkley left Kansas for Texas.

From that "fine flying field in Del Rio" Brinkley's airplanes were dispatched over and over again "airlifting those in search of their true potential" to Brinkley's front door.

For whatever the ailment, Brinkley had a cure.

"This treatment can make old men execute young ideas," he warmly advertised over his radio station XERA which he had conveniently built just across the Rio Grande in Mexico to avoid any encounter with the U. S. federal communications folks.

He was without question a master of finesse on the radio. Combining equal doses of homey philosophy, gardening advice and flamboyant medical terminology with a thorough mixture of fundamental religion, Brinkley gained the trust of an audience who had never heard of Del Rio, much less considered the possibility of flying there in an airplane.

"Not to worry if you don't know your way down here to our little town," he would drone comfortingly. "I'll just send my airplane on a mission of mercy to pick you up and bring you for a little visit."

Brinkley branched over into Arkansas, which many say was his undoing. Eventually, the postal authorities arrested him for illegal use of the mail to solicit funds. Pressured by the American

Medical Society, Brinkley's credentials were finally exposed as "unverifiable."

He escaped conviction by dying in 1942. On his deathbed he continued to declare himself, his radio station and his airplane as "saviors who will be vindicated in the years to come."

The obvious question is "did it work?"

From the standpoint of pure science, there is now no medical basis or evidence to believe goat glands can make men virile. But Brinkley garnered hundreds of testimonials from those who left Del Rio aboard the Lockheed swearing that everything the doctor had promised had come true. Many even sent photos of bouncing baby boys—not too surprisingly most were named "John" or "Billy" in grateful appreciation.

The fact cannot be denied that John R. Brinkley sold the one thing people needed most: Hope.

No evidence exists to indicate Brinkley was a licensed pilot or ever actually flew his own airplanes. But then a man who would perform goat gland transplants without completing medical school would probably have felt no need to be bothered with such a minor matter as obtaining a valid pilot's license.

So closely entwined were aviation and Brinkley in Texas that it was said anytime a silver shape appeared overhead folks would cock an eye skyward and say, "There comes Dr. Brinkley!" Airports and airstrips sprang up overnight in order to accommodate the Texas "angel of mercy." Some have passed into oblivion or fallen to shambles like the old Brinkley mansion in Del Rio that recently has been salvaged and restored. Some, however, have become part of today's thriving Texas airport system.

Was John R. Brinkley the father of Texas' medical airlift services for organ transplants, a medical charlatan or a miracle visionary?

As the good doctor would say to those considering the Average Man's Treatment, "The choice, dear friend, is entirely up to you."

These warriors have gone on to ride the Unseen Realm.
Courtesy Institute of Texan Cultures

8

Inconspicuous Gallantry

When the great epic of the West is written, this is one of the wild notes that must sound in it. —Frederic Remington

---

Mama was a firm believer in doing your duty. She inherited that firm belief from her mother, Elva Macon.

My grandfather Ebb called my grandmother "The Madam."

The Madam hated that nickname, but Lord, how she loved Ebb Macon. Even when he took up with the Cafe Woman, who took him for almost everything he had.

What the Cafe Woman didn't get, the Internal Revenue Service did.

Ebb Macon was a good man in many ways. He worked hard. He didn't smoke. He didn't drink liquor.

He just didn't believe in giving his hard earned money to the government.

He did, however, believe in paying wages and women in cash.

Daddy always said it was George Moore who turned Ebb in to the IRS after Ebb nearly ran over George with the winch truck while they were moving a house.

Mama said it was the Cafe Woman who did it.

The Madam said the tithe belonged to the Lord, even if He had to use the IRS to collect.

Ebb didn't go to jail but sometimes I think he wished he had. After the IRS got through with him there wasn't any cash left to pay wages. Or women.

Long after I was a woman myself, I asked Mama why my grandmother put up with my grandfather's affairs.

"Love and duty go together," she said. "Some people just love enough to do more duty than others."

———————

Brackettville, Texas, is the home of the World Tortilla Tossing Tournament.

It is also the home of Alamo Village, a motion picture filming location, and the recreational retirement community of Fort Clark Springs, which was once a Cavalry outpost.

Don't plan to fly in for any of these Brackettville attractions, because the one thing Brackettville *does not* have is a municipal airport. Several private strips dot the 1,359 square miles of Kinney County but smart pilots know you do not land at any strip marked "private" on the sectional map without having made prior arrangements.

Del Rio is only 30 miles to the west, so a smart pilot lands there and borrows a car for the drive over to Brackettville to catch a tortilla and to walk down the streets of the movie set where John Wayne made history.

Few tourists, however, come to Brackettville to visit Seminole Cemetery.

This cemetery could look like any other plot of a hundred mounds along the outskirts of a small town, except for one thing: noticeable from the road are four white tombstones surrounded by four iron fences scattered among the hand-scraped markers and rough wooden crosses.

Except for the names and ranks, the four white tombstones read the same:

MEDAL OF HONOR
INDIAN SCOUTS
INDIAN WARS

Pompey Factor was a private.
So was Adam Paine.
John Ward was a sergeant.
Young Isaac Payne was a trumpeter.

That four Medal of Honor recipients should all be buried in a small cemetery four miles south of Brackettville, Texas, is unusual. That all four were honored for their service in the period of the Indian wars is even more unusual.

What is incredible, however, is that *all four of these heroes were black*. Of the 3,412 who have been honored with the highest U. S. military decoration for "conspicious gallantry and intrepidity at the risk of life, above and beyond the call of duty," only 78 are black.

The four buried in the Seminole Cemetery were part of the hardest-hitting and most decorated military unit ever placed in the field by the United States. The "Seminole Negro Indian Scouts," as they are known in the U.S. War Department records, were descendants of slave runaways who had settled among the Seminole tribes in Florida before the War Between the States.

Removed to the Indian Territories, they later migrated to Mexico where they faced repeated attempts to re-enslave them. Then in 1870, General Zenas Bliss of the U.S. Army, in his desperation for scouts in the mounting campaigns against the Plains Indian tribes, went to Mexico to promise land and food to any of the Seminoles who would serve as U.S. Army Scouts.

Many scorned the scouting unit Bliss formed until encounters with the unit proved the scouts were superb trackers and fighters. Placed under the command of Lieutenant John Bullis (who was white) and assigned to various cavalry and infantry units, the Seminole Scouts never lost a man in nine years of battle, nor even had one seriously wounded.

On April 25, 1875, Bullis, with three of his black scouts—Ward, Payne and Factor—attacked a party of 30 Comanches attempting to cross the Pecos River. In the Comanches' counterattack, Bullis lost his horse and the Indians swept toward him.

"We can't leave the Lieutenant, boys," Ward shouted, and raced back to Bullis. Payne and Factor galloped after him, firing into the charging Indians, and Bullis was saved.

A later act of valor by Adam Paine in rescuing his fellow scouts brought the number of Congressional honorees among the Seminoles to four.

But Texas was not afterward kind to the Seminoles, and the federal government's promises of food and property were left empty.

Outlaws killed two of the scouts. Paine, accused in Florida of a knife slaying, was shot in the back by a Texas sheriff from such close range that it set his clothes on fire.

Factor and a small band washed the dust of Texas from their horses' hooves and rode back into Mexico. The unit disintegrated after that, finally disbanding in 1881.

About a hundred Seminole Scouts are buried in the cemetery that lies a few miles south of Fort Clark. Men like John Bowlegs, Ben July, George Kibbit, Billie Wilson and Renty Grayson are among those named on the historical marker. The names of others aren't even known.

Four Medal of Honor tombstones with their simple white fences are all that remind passersby of four black men who individually surmounted horrible racial prejudice and injustice to serve a country that would no longer care for them when their heroism was done.

There are no ceremonies, parades or memorial services at Seminole Cemetery this third Monday in January. Only one lost pilot in search of a Brackettville tortilla.

It is late and the wind is shifting. There is just enough time to drive the 30 miles back to Del Rio and get airborne before the cold front pushes through.

"The Seminoles believe these warriors have gone on to ride the Unseen Realm on misty steeds, scouting the starry plains above to defend us from enemies more relentless and terrible than flesh and blood," wrote a Brackettville Seminole descendant.

If you depart Del Rio and hear what you think is thunder, do not be alarmed.

It is only young Isaac Payne, Medal of Honor Seminole Indian Scout, blowing his trumpet to lead you safely through the skies.

The American planes...prettiest sight I ever saw.

9

Gestapo Guests

Let them be forgotten who will not remember. —Black Elk of the Oglala
Sioux

He was an old man, well into his eighties.

He stood, very dignified, outside the door of the Royal Air
Force Museum at Hendon, occasionally blowing into his hands to
warm them in the London chill.

Wearing a woolen sweater and scarf, he presented the perfect
picture of an aged Englishman who had lived and worked many
years in the potato fields of East Anglia.

He was selling War Remembrance Poppies. In England, the
Armistice is celebrated concurrently with our Veterans Day.

"Would you buy a poppy, mum?" he politely asked.

"Of course. I'll keep it as a souvenir of my trip," I replied in
my Texas nasal twang that branded me a foreigner.

The old man's eyes came to life and his politeness melted away
as his trembling hand reached out, took my hand and lifted it to
his lips, where he kissed my fingers.

"You are an American," he said with a quiver. "I had lost
everything in the war except my life. Then the Americans came
and saved me from a fate that would have been worse then
death."

He kissed my hand again, pressed a poppy into my palm, and turned to hide his face as tears spilled down the crevices of time etched on his cheeks.

Over the Brenner Pass the B-24 Liberator began taking flak.

The young man in the crew radio-gunner's position was a long way from his hometown of Baird, Texas, where folks affectionately knew him as "Buddy." Buddy had graduated from high school there, then had three years of college at nearby Abilene Christian before enlisting to serve his country in a war destined to forever change history. . . and his life.

During his days in Baird, Buddy never dreamed that he would be heading for Czechoslovakia on a bitterly cold day in February of 1944. Nor did he, like thousands of others, ever imagine he was heading for an enemy prison camp.

It happened quickly. The German fighters finished off the B-24, and Buddy bailed out into enemy territory, hoping to make it to Yugoslavia and back to Allied lines.

The Gestapo had other plans. Captured in a barn in the German countryside, West Texas boy Buddy Hart became a prisoner of war. He would spend 15 months in Nazi "hospitality": Stalag Luft 6, Stalag Luft 4. . . and the infamous Stalag Luft 1.

He was not alone.

Stalag Luft 1, otherwise known as "Barth on the Baltic," was also home to three Abilene High School graduates. One had worked as a newsboy for the *Abilene Reporter-News;* one had attended Texas A & M as a cadet; one was a mail clerk for West Texas Utilities. Like Hart, all three became crew members on airplanes flying from bases in the European Theater.

Connell Taylor was a B-17 instructor pilot who had bailed out over Magdeburg, Germany, when flak got the number two engine and the wing caught fire.

R. C. Fry was a B-26 instructor who had flown 56 missions before ME-410's got one engine and all of his plane's elevator controls on a night mission over Northern France. He got out at 400 feet.

Earl Hoppe's B-24 was on fire. He had a hole in his leg big enough to poke a fist through, but he got out south of Hanover—three of his fellow crew members didn't.

Though captured at different times and in different locations, the three found themselves at Stalag Luft 1 with Buddy Hart.

They had not seen each other since their school days in West Texas.

Germany wasn't the only place American prisoners of war struggled to survive. Across the Pacific in the Philippines, China, Burma, and Japan, men and women found themselves enduring heat, humidity and inhuman torture at the hands of their captors. Marine or foot soldier, each like Buddy Hart and the others at Stalag 1 dreamed of coming home.

Some made it. Many did not.

In Korea and especially in Vietnam, the term "prisoner of war" became even more ominous as liberation of American prisoners seemed no longer to be a priority and "winning" wasn't the objective. For those who had been World War II POWs the thing they had thought impossible happened: American prisoners of war were left behind when the fighting was over.

Such was not the case in the spring of 1945 when Stalag 1 was liberated.

"The American planes came in and picked us up. It was the prettiest sight I ever saw," Fry remembers.

Hart, Taylor, Hoppe and Fry all have vivid memories of life as a POW. in Germany.

"Cold and hungry. Always. We were given three small potatoes each day—that was it. Sometimes we might get a bowl of turnip soup or some dehydrated sauerkraut but not often," Fry describes their diet.

"We were entitled to a Red Cross parcel once a week," Hart says. "But we never got them—maybe once a month if we were lucky. The Germans took everything. We found out later they were absolutely desperate. But they made us think they were in great shape."

A typical Red Cross parcel contained corned beef, powdered milk, margarine, salmon, raisins, biscuits, cheese, sugar cubes, a ration chocolate "D" bar, soap and cigarettes.

Kriegies (as POWs were known in the Stalags) would carefully divide up a little packet of raisins and make them last for days by eating one at a time.

Unforgettable was the black bread made of sawdust with coal tar margarine.

"It had so much sawdust it didn't mold—it just turned into board," Hoppe says with a laugh.

Forty years after Stalag Luft 1 it is easy to laugh. But not to forget. When they were returned to the United States each went a different direction, but eventually all four came back to Abilene.

"We hadn't seen each other in a number of years," Fry says. "Connell came by my house to invite me to go to the meeting of the local chapter of American Ex-POWs with him. I hardly recognized him. Of course we all have a lot in common, but we don't just sit around and rehash the terrible things that happened."

The chapter strongly advocates the accountability of all considered "missing in action" or "prisoner of war."

Waitresses in the restaurant meeting room say the Ex-POW group is a special pleasure to serve. "They don't waste food," one says.

"It was a very difficult and a very special time in our lives," Dr. Harry L. Haynes of Stamford tells audiences to whom he presents programs about "the Shoe Leather Express," the 86-day march of the POWs from German prison camps in advance of the Russian winter offensive in 1945.

"We held together when the whole world around us was falling apart."

While they had no bullets, POWs battled the enemy even in the confines of the camps.

"The guards had dogs which were constantly jumping us and would have killed us if told to. I would grind up a powdered milk can and feed it to the dogs with my food—it was worth starving to know I was keeping the dog from killing one of us," Hart says, sharing one of the grim stores of survival. "I liked dogs, but this was different."

Taylor recalls the more light-hearted times. "I remember getting to take a shower—we only got two while I was there. I'd forgotten how good I could smell."

On the first Tuesday of the month when the West Central Texas Chapter of American Ex-Prisoners of War meet, it is doubtful any have gone more than 24 hours without a shower. But the scars soap and water cannot wash away are still visible. Some walk with a noticeable limp, some cannot stand straight, some can barely hear.

None try to call attention to their difficulties.

"We're the lucky ones and we know it," a balding, former Marine fighter pilot explains.

Buddy Hart's mother kept a scrapbook of his experiences. It includes clippings from the newspaper reporting him as killed in action, numerous pieces of correspondence concerning his capture and placement in prison camp, and a crudely made "dogtag" with his POW number "1831" scratched by hand at Stalag Luft 6.

Then there is the yellowed Western Union paper dated June 16, 1945:

The Chief of Staff of the Army directs me to inform you your son, T/Sgt Jesse C. Hart is being returned to the United States within the near future and will be given an opportunity to communicate with you upon arrival.

Ex-prisoner of war Buddy Hart was coming home.

Bonnie had a special charm...something to do with the sadness that flickered in her eyes even when she smiled.

10

Hoodoo Woman

"Marie Laveau? Sure I heard of her. I don't know if she was good or bad; folks says both ways. But I know this: she was a very powerful woman. I saw her once jump up in the air and go whizzing out the door and over the top of the telephone wires.

"Sometimes now if folks in the Quarter see a tall, dark-haired woman wearin' white they thinks its Marie a-fixin' to go flyin' again. Don't mess with a woman like Marie or she'll put the hoodoo on you." —From the book *Voodoo in New Orleans* by Robert Tallant

---

Mama always feared I would grow up to be like Bonnie, one of Daddy's sisters.

Bonnie was tall and willowy with Cherokee cheekbones, a slender waist and broad hips that made men weak with anticipation.

Bonnie also had a special charm that attracted old women and little kids to her as well as lonely men. I think it had something to do with the sadness that flickered in her eyes even when she smiled.

Everybody loved Bonnie. Including Mama.

Everybody wasn't enough for Bonnie. She had a passion she tried to satisfy by marrying men she didn't love and loving men she didn't marry. She always wore a pearl broach locket full of perfume and carried a purse full of pills.

Heart problems, she told us.

One Christmas Bonnie gave me a pair of red cowgirl boots. She told Mama she paid for them working for a rich Chicago cattle buyer at the Stockyards in Fort Worth.

Mama said you had to admire Bonnie for being honest. But she never did let me wear those boots.

"Bonnie paid too much for them," she would explain each time I begged her to take them down off the top shelf of the closet where she had hidden them away.

It wasn't until I was old enough to know the truth about Bonnie's working career in the Stockyards' houses of ill repute that I understood what Mama meant about the price Bonnie paid for those boots.

Finally, there were too many men. Too many pills. Too many heartaches. Mama took one look at Bonnie in her coffin and turned as white as Daddy's shirt.

"Oh, Hubert," Mama sobbed on Daddy's arm, "Nancy looks just like her."

I was only seven, but the long legs and the Cherokee cheekbones were already evident. There wasn't anything broad about me then, however, except my knee caps.

I thought Bonnie looked beautiful lying there wearing her black silk dress and imitation pearl broach. You couldn't tell one of the pearls was missing unless you looked real close.

I asked Mama if I could have pink roses on my coffin just like Bonnie had on hers.

That's when Doris Kinney had to help Mama to a chair and the church ladies had to fan her with wet cloths.

I just kept looking at Bonnie wondering why everyone was crying so hard when she looked so happy.

From the corner balcony above the intersection of Bourbon and Orleans Street you hear and smell the sunset in New Orleans as much as you see it. Honky-tonk jazz and Creole/Cajun music compete for the tourists who throng the sidewalks while whiffs of shrimp and oysters liquor the air with intoxicating aromas.

Evening deepens into dark and the old French Quarter throbs to life.

Just above my room in the elegantly restored Bourbon Orleans hotel is the historic Orleans Ballroom. It was built in 1815 to cater to the city's insatiable love for dancing and entertainment. Masquerades and even the notorious Quadroon Balls were held here. Almost two hundred years ago I might have been swooning to the attention of Creole gentlemen bidding for my favors in a time and circumstance that made old New Orleans a world to itself—a world that is now a scant four hours away from West Texas when your airplane's compass heading reads 110 degrees.

Singer Tom T. Hall made the infamous Marie Laveau known to a generation of music fans who had never before heard of the most powerful voodoo queen who "ruled" New Orleans for almost eighty years. While Hall's song hit the Top-10 charts across the country, it actually told little of the real Marie Laveau.

With an airplane and a few days in New Orleans I would search out the mystery of this woman to whom I'd felt strangely akin ever since I had played the part of her in a theater production 20 years before.

Marie Laveau was a mixture of Negro, Indian and white bloods. She was described as a tall, statuesque woman with curling black hair, "good" features, dark skin that had a distinctly reddish cast and fierce black eyes. Both she and her husband, Jacques Paris, were free people of color.

Voodoo was thriving in New Orleans in 1819 when Marie and Jacques were married. They lived in what is now the 1900 block of North Rampart Street. Marie endeared herself to the Catholic parish where she helped the priest care for victims of Yellow Fever.

Later she gained entrance into the homes of the wealthy as a hairdresser and became the confidante of both men and women, black and white, Creole and Quadroon.

Mysteriously, Jacques disappeared a short while after their marriage. Soon Marie took a lover by the name of Louis Christophe Glapion, who had fought in the Battle of New Orleans. It was after Glapion came that Marie Laveau arose to be a queen among those who mixed orthodox Christianity and spiritual mysticism to produce a form of worship known as voodoo.

To this confusion Marie added a great deal of shrewd business savvy to become New Orleans' most feared Voodoo Queen.

Whether it was a girl desperate to attract a young man's fancy, a man eager to eliminate his business competition or a matron suspicious of her husband's waning attentions, Marie Laveau had the solution. To her home poured a steady stream of New Orleans' socially elite in search of the magic they heard she had the power to do.

A young girl would be told to bring Marie the glove of the man she loved. This would be filled with a mixture of steel dust, sugar and honey—the sugar and honey were to "sweeten" the man, the steel dust was for power over him—and the girl was instructed to sleep with the glove under her mattress. Within three days he would be in her control. If not, Marie would vow that the man was "tainted" and the girl should have no part of him.

It was, however, the belief that Marie Laveau could fly that brought her the greatest esteem as a Voodoo Queen.

How else, reasoned those who secretly sought her charms and potions, could this voodoo woman know so quickly and so well what transpired within the walls of their private lives? Reports circulated throughout New Orleans that Madam Laveau had been seen wearing a white gown swishing above the heads of those on whom she wished to put a hex.

Or cure of a malady.

Or free from an evil spirit.

Of course it was Marie's connections among the servants in the homes of her clients who constantly fed her with facts and secrets told only in the boudoirs of the elite Garden District. With her keen intelligence and having the ability to read and write (powers even some of her wealthiest clients did not possess) Marie was always in demand when it came to "making hoodoo."

The first Marie Laveau died in 1881, and old New Orleans mourned the passing of "a sainted spiritual woman."

One of the fifteen children born to Marie and Glapion became the second Marie Laveau after her mother's death. She is said to have been her mother's image, only slightly taller and with a much harder heart and an even more clever mind.

"The daughter lives her mother again," they chanted on St. John's Eve. And like her mother, they said, the new Marie Laveau could fly. In fact, one of the ways she reportedly got rid of unwelcome people was to write their name on a balloon and release it in the direction she wanted them to go as she flew above the graveyard.

From the gruesome to the outlandish, the stories of Marie Laveau captivated the imaginations of three generations of New Orleans residents. Some thought she should be hung as a witch; others petitioned the Church to make her a saint. Children were taught never to look at her, while men were unable to take their eyes off of her when she presided over a "spiritual gathering."

No one knows for sure how the daughter Marie Laveau died. She had drifted into obscurity as new voodoo queens gained control. But after her death she was reportedly seen on numerous occasions flying in her white gown. She was said to be always looking for tall, dark-haired women to give them "the Power."

Ah! Could it be that it was Marie Laveau who cast this spell on me of wanting to "jump in the air and go whizzing out the door and flying over telephone lines?" If so, dear readers, you would do well to remember the advice of the folks down in the old French Quarter:

"Don't mess with a woman like Marie. She'll put the hoodoo on you."

11

Burning Memories

Who among us shall dwell with the devouring fire? —Isaiah 33:14

In spite of Mama's best efforts I still made my share of mistakes. Though I never rode the rails with the Fort Worth Stockyards cowboys I did, in a way, grow up to be like Bonnie.

The difference is that I have a passion to give pleasure with words on a piece of paper. It began when I was three with a red crayon on our living room wallpaper.

When Mama saw what I had done she firmly impressed on me that I was not to use the wallpaper for my creative endeavors. She would not, however, let Daddy cover over that scribble when he re-wallpapered the living room in '55. She said someday I was going to be a famous writer and she wanted to be able to show people my first *publication.*

While Mama waited for someday, I pursued a variety of careers—everything from picking potatoes to helping executives who couldn't spell Pocatella get promoted up the organizational ladder.

Each time one of those corporate climbers asked me what I planned to be doing in five years when he became President of the company, I said I did not plan to be working for him.

They usually laughed.

I kept writing.

On grocery sacks, on bread wrappers, even inside the soles of my shoes. There was so much around me others didn't see...

Sounds no one else seemed to hear...

Feelings begging to be painted with words on my canvas of tablet paper.

Like the disappearing dust of a perfect crosswind landing on a moonlit night;

Like the deafening silence of a prop suddenly stopped in midair;

Like the trembling fingers of an old man too proud to cry.

Now they make crayons soap and water can wash off your livingroom wallpaper without leaving a trace of scribble.

Too bad.

Someday a lot of mamas are going to be sorry.

———————————

A thousand feet above Shackelford County we watched West Texas burn.

For as far as the smoke would let us see, the land lay black like a scorched corduroy skirt. We turned to stay upwind of the smoke and watched the tongues of fire lap into what was left of the brown pastures.

My lone passenger was silent. With the cold front's passage leaving rough air behind, the airplane bumped and bucked regularly, making conversation inconvenient at best, and impossible at times.

But it wasn't the ride that kept us both silent.

It wasn't the rough air that made my stomach heavy.

It was the look in the old rancher's face that settled sick inside my jaws.

It wasn't just his land that was on fire...

It was 77 years of his life.

Years ago he'd left the homeplace and moved to town. The tired house he left behind had weathered as brown as the pasture, and dilapidation had set in with a vengeance. The Herefords had stomped the front porch until only the frame remained of the flooring.

Broomweed had replaced the welcome mat.

But the polished porcelain doorknob still waited in the front door for one last guest to give it a turn.

The shed where the kids had ridden stick horses had fared better. Feed stored there was still easy to get to even if the rain washed out most of the road.

Rain.

As promising as the idea might sound, the man with dust from the Depression still deep in his craw feared what others could not understand. Too much rain, too hard a rain, too late or too soon a rain and the land would be devastated again.

He waved toward the billow of smoke.

He wanted a last look.

The cattle were bunched together at the creek on the only patch of green surrounded by black. They watched the airplane circle and bellowed in a frightened daze. All that had saved them was the shift of the wind.

Unable to move from where it had stood for nearly a hundred years, the house had taken on the fire as bravely as it could. Flames poured through glassless window frames and danced eerily along the hanging gutters. A jackrabbit darted frantically from the chimney rocks scattered by the side door.

Only the livingroom wall was standing.

His hands gave him away. He never blinked, his back never bent. But his nine and a half fingers dug into his khakied knees so tightly his elbows quivered.

We made a one-eighty overhead just as the roof collapsed.

From north of Clyde to the Clear Fork, black smoke from tank batteries and burning oil like lava flows painted grotesque shapes on the horizon.

He said he was glad *she* hadn't lived to see this.

I nodded and didn't answer. What do you say to a man whose memories just went up in smoke?

Albany's Hickman Field Airport was beginning to fill with other aircraft coming to view the remains.

We rolled to a stop on the ramp. When I told him I couldn't accept pay for the flight he insisted he wanted to return the favor. So I told him if he had an old porcelain doorknob he didn't need, I'd call it even.

He allowed that he might.

I asked if I could write about flying him over his ranch. About the old homeplace. About the fire.

He said he'd rather I wouldn't.

I was planning to keep it our secret as he'd asked. Then I heard a young greenhorn news announcer say the worst range fire in the history of West Texas had caused no "serious" injuries to anyone.

Little does he know.

12

"Get Villa!"

The history of the operations of the 1st Aero Squadron in this Mexican campaign would fill a large-sized book. —B. D. Foulois, Major General, USAF (ret.)

I stole a piece of jalapeno bubble gum from the Williams' neighborhood grocery store. Theda Westfall, who worked at the cash register, saw me do it. She let me know if she caught me doing it again I would be forbidden entrance into the store.

That was all the conviction I needed to repent of my sin.

Once a week I got a nickel to spend. I would go to sleep each night dreaming of what I was going to buy and how delicious it was going to taste when I was sitting in front of the store with the other kids devouring my treat.

A cherry Popsicle...a chocolate candy bar...a pink peanut patty.

Sometimes I dreamed of reaching into the red Coca-Cola cooler box, pulling out an ice cold bottle, popping the cap off in the opener and turning it up for a swig like I saw the big kids do. But that took six cents, and an extra penny was something I could seldom come by.

What I loved most about the grocery store was the big poster that hung on the wall behind the cooler box. It was a World War II tribute to "the Aviatrix" and featured a beautiful girl wearing a helmet with goggles standing in front of a shiny radial airplane engine. "Your thirst takes wings" was splashed above the propeller in bright, bold letters.

On the days I had no nickel to spend I would simply stand by the cooler box and imagine I was the beautiful girl in the poster who could fly.

Cheap thrills for a kid who didn't even own a tricycle.

No piece of jalapeno bubble gum was worth losing my grocery store privileges. I figured I had better tell Mama before Theda did that I was a bubble gum bandit who had been caught in the act.

"I am so disappointed in you," was all Mama said.

She was standing at the kitchen sink and wouldn't look at me.

The way she said it made me wish I had never seen jalapeno bubble gum. Then she set the punishment to fit the crime.

"For the next four weeks you have to buy jalapeno bubble gum with each of your nickels."

I thought I had gotten off easy until the third week when it was July hot and I desperately wanted a cherry Popsicle.

Mama would not budge.

"I won't always be around to make sure you do the right thing. You must learn to make the right decisions or suffer the consequences."

He watched us carefully with steel-squinted eyes as we taxied the Piper Aztec airplane to a stop. There wasn't a speck of shade or a breath of air in the midday sun scalding the Lajitas Airport.

We parked where horses were once stabled for General John "Blackjack" Pershing's cavalry troops. More than a half century has passed since Pershing came to this post on the Rio Grande determined almost to insanity to capture the infamous bandit Pancho Villa...

More than half a century, but the Mexican has not forgotten.

He loaded us into his rusted station wagon and hauled us up the hill to the Badlands Hotel—careful to remind us twice to be sure the airplane was tied down securely.

"The wind may blow wild tonight," he said.

Then he threw his head back and laughed crazily.

"You are planning to ride the river. . . to canoe the rapids through the canyons?" he asked.

We said yes—that was why we had come to Lajitas.

He laughed again, that crazy laughter men have when they know secrets they are anxious to tell.

Lajitas is a Spanish name meaning "flat rocks." To get there from here you travel west—so far west in Texas that you move not only in miles but in time. In just over two hours in the Aztec we had stepped into yesterday without ever leaving today.

Located 17 miles west of Terlingua, Lajitas on the Rio Grande lies across the river from Mexico amid 30,000 acres of the most magnificent, rugged country humanity ever set eyes or feet on.

Some will argue that there isn't anything west of Terlingua except tequila and tarantulas. Now known only for its yearly chili cookoffs, Terlingua is officially listed on the map as a ghost town.

Such was not always the case. Once it was a raucous boom town where the search for quicksilver made blood and emotions run red-hot.

The Mexican followed us into the Lajitas saloon, where the refrigerated cooling brought us back to life again. It was plain he wanted to talk, so we told him to pull up a chair and order on us.

"Tourists want to hear about Terlingua. No one cares about Lajitas," he began.

Miners discovered cinnabar lying on top of the ground or only a few inches under the surface of Terlingua. Mercury was unbelievably easy to extract and at the turn of the century was in strong demand in the marketplace because of its usefulness as a gunpowder detonator. By 1902 a "mother lode" area at Terlingua stretched 40 miles long and 20 miles wide. Millions of dollars worth of mercury was mined under the auspices of the Chisos Mining Company.

"After the end of World War II, Terlingua died," the Mexican said wryly. "Today it is mostly rabbits and red sand."

Then he waved his hand toward the saloon door.

"But out there. . . now there is some *real* history."

History, yes. But otherwise, Lajitas is so remote from civilization that there seems to be little else. There isn't a post office or a hospital. The nearest doctor is a hundred miles up the road. The closest thing to a "convenience" store is the original Lajitas Trading Post where you can still exchange live chickens for canned tomatoes and "light" bread.

You have to wait your turn, of course. While doing so you can lean against the old adobe walls in the shade along with the rest of the customers who arrive at the trading post on foot, in dilapidated pickups or by mule.

"You have heard of Villa—Pancho Villa?" he asked hoarsely, leaning closer to the table.

We said yes, that we had. Villa, the Mexican bandit general led the Mexican attack on Columbus, New Mexico on March 19, 1916. The United States retaliated by sending Pershing in pursuit.

"Then you know they never caught him?"

We said yes. And we leaned closer to the table.

"It was in the canyons along the Rio Grande here at Lajitas where Villa and his men hid out. . . watch tomorrow when you pass that third rapid. You will see a trail leading into the mountains. A half mile into the pass you'll find an old rock house. It was Villa's. I'm sure!"

Pershing's search for Villa brought about an event that forever changed history. He became obsessed with bringing Villa to justice, and his obsession brought to life the first actual use of aircraft by Americans in "guerrilla" warfare. The airplanes of the 1st Aero Squadron were to be Pershing's eyes and ears. They would "roam far and wide, discover Villa," and direct troops to converge for "the kill."

"But it did not work that way. The crates cracked up in flight or were driven down by the wind currents into the trees. . . the American government made Pershing stop the whole thing. . . and Villa was never captured!"

The Mexican's eyes were wide with excitement.

"Just think, my friends. Your one airplane could have done what Pershing and all his troops could not. They could not find Villa."

He ordered another frosted root beer.

"It angers me," his voice quivered, "that some silly chili cookoff war in Terlingua gets more attention than Lajitas. People should know about Lajitas, where the great Pancho Villa escaped under Pershing's very nose!"

He began to laugh again.

"No one knows what happened to Villa. . . except me. I know."

He fixed his eyes past the oval glass in the saloon door toward the rocky cemetery on the hill below the town. There was not a sound in the saloon, except for the expectant breathing of his listeners.

"Villa is here. . ."

Abruptly he pushed back from the table and was gone.

Out in Lajitas, they say the nights are so crystal clear you'll be able to see stars you never saw at home. But on the nights when there happens to be an airplane parked on the ramp of the airstrip where Pershing's horses once were stabled, the wind comes howling through the canyons and the dirt blows like bullets, shaking even the old adobe buildings.

Some believe it is Pershing's spirit trying to fly again.

Others say it is Pancho's laughter from an unmarked grave nearby.

Only the Mexican knows for sure. And he's not telling.

The old man in the right seat.

13

Racing Leonard Crow Dog

She'll be comin' round the mountain when she comes. —Railroad ballad of the 1880s

---

One of the most difficult things for instructors to teach student pilots is that once something unplanned occurs, something else will usually go wrong in your flight.

Lose an engine on takeoff and a power line you never saw before will suddenly appear straight ahead;

Lose your radios and the need to communicate will immediately become critical;

Lose your self-control and panic will set in like bubble gum on shoe leather.

Bill Masters, who has been teaching people to fly since I was a kid slurping cherry Popsicles in front of Williams' grocery store, always makes his students deal with multiple emergencies during their training.

Nothing ever happens in ones, he warns.

Then he smoothly closes the throttle of the Piper Aztec's left engine as you are descending to traffic pattern altitude.

Next he informs you the gear won't extend, so if you are going to have wheels underneath you when you encounter the runway you had better start working the manual hydraulic pump *now*.

Whatever you do, he insists, hold your heading and hold your airspeed.

You are sweating puddles in the Aztec's left seat, but the runway is in sight. You have it made...you think.

The air traffic controller says "November 717 Echo, go around."

What? He must be kidding.

Do you tell him you can't, that you are going to have to land anyway? Or do you try to do as he says?

Why doesn't the old man in the right seat with 13,000 hours of experience tell you what to do? An agony of seconds passes before something in the back of your mind comes sharply into focus:

The instructor isn't going to do it for you!

Making your own choice and accepting the responsibility for the results of that choice are what this whole lesson has been about!

Even the controller was in on Masters' lesson plan to teach you pilot stress management. Now both of them are waiting on you to do the right thing.

Push the throttles full open.

Verify left engine out.

Flaps up.

Feather.

Gear up. (Pump, Nancy, as if your life depends upon it because this time it does.)

Maintain single engine climb speed.

Head for Elmdale's traffic pattern.

Complete the before landing checklist.

Lesson over.

"I won't always be around to make sure you do the right thing," the old man says as the two of you push the Aztec into the hangar. "You must learn to make the right decision or suffer the consequences."

Lord, have mercy.

Mama and Bill Masters must have been cut from the same bubble-gum wrapper.

———————

For a flatlander from Texas taking off from the airport at Rifle, Colorado, there is an immediate feeling of excitement. . . and uneasiness.

To get to Texas your course must turn south and stay west of the mountains, unless you can quickly climb to 14,000 feet to clear Crested Butte.

The Cessna 206 does not climb that quickly. Not when it is carrying 1,500 pounds of people, fishing tackle, cold weather gear, toolboxes and 40 pounds of freshly caught Colorado trout from the lake at Ripple Creek Pass.

It had been a fun four days roughing it in a two-room cabin sans plumbing, where the electricity shuts off promptly at 10 each evening and kicks back on no earlier than 6 the next morning. It doesn't matter because by then you're already somewhere on the Colorado River tempting the "cutthroats" with your fly lures.

Chances are good that you missed morning coffee because it will hardly boil at this altitude. Especially over the wood cook stove. And the mosquitoes don't wait until dark to bite, so you smell of repellant and don't bother to wash your hair every day.

Ah, wilderness.

We had tried to leave Rifle the previous morning, but Leonard Crow Dog had made it impossible. Crow Dog is the Sioux medicine man who makes rain. He had been called in by Midwest farmers in a final attempt to entreat Divine Providence to bring an end to the drought devouring the country.

Three times a day Crow Dog conducted his ancient rainmaking ceremonies in a location, and then moved on.

He had not failed in 127 previous rainmaking attempts and yesterday in Rifle was no exception.

The forecast was good this morning. At least for the expected five hours we would need to get home. But early afternoon and evening storms across the mountains ahead of us were expected.

Crow Dog was moving our direction. The time to go was now.

In spite of the fact we weren't climbing as fast as we should, I felt good. Almost smug. But the nagging gnaw of suspicion that all was not right became fact when we turned east at Blue Mesa Reservoir.

The 206 had a bad magneto.

Could be the switch.

Could be a bad wire.

Could be a problem.

However, there were airports all along the way and once we got over the mountains from Gunnison to Saguahe it would be smooth terrain and open territory.

Once we got over the mountains.

"Reminds me a lot of the Palo Duro Canyon area," my unsuspecting passenger commented. Little did she know the last thing I wanted to be reminded of over this last stretch of Old West hideouts was Palo Duro Canyon. My memory was still vividly clear of looking down into the Texas Panhandle canyon and then up to an airplane windshield rapidly becoming covered with oil.

A duster pilot strip saved us two years ago from having to land with a broken crankshaft in Palo Duro Canyon. But there weren't any duster pilot strips on top of these mountains.

"I wouldn't want to see any oil on the windshield here," I tell her, noting the clouds are moving much quicker now and the rain showers in the canyons are more frequent.

Deja vu.

Is that rain on the windshield? Or is it oil? Am I imagining those little droplets or are they real?

Surely my mind is playing tricks on me.

This can't be happening *again*.

The oily blur on the windshield confirms that it is.

I watch the lightning in a thundershower 10 miles away and wonder how long you can live on trout in the middle of nowhere at 11,000 feet.

Leonard Crow Dog's lightning laughs again.

What would my old instructor do? The answers flash from my memory like Crow Dog's lightning:

Fly the airplane.

Hold altitude and hold course for Alamosa and hope the oil pressure doesn't drop.

Watch for flat breaks between the trees, always calculating the wind, the angles and the glide.

Make sure the shoulder harness is snug.

Tighten the seatbelt.

Trust the line drawn on the sectional map that shows Alamosa straight ahead.

Fly the airplane.

We cleared the runway and rolled to a stop with left windshield visibility good. The right side was another story.

It was my turn to laugh at Leonard Crow Dog when the problem turned out to be a failed crankshaft seal, and not the crankshaft itself. With any luck we'd be on our way ahead of him within the hour. With the weather building between us and Texas it would be none too soon at that.

I did not laugh for long.

There is an old saying in aviation that you should never let anything mechanical know you are in a hurry. The magneto we thought to be repaired proved otherwise during engine run-up so we taxied back for three more hours in the Alamosa maintenance hangar.

When we were finally on our way we had to zigzag around a dozen rain showers scattered along either side of the Rio Grande.

Crow Dog was now definitely in the lead.

The pass at Taos was full of sirens luring us to try our luck threading between its mist-covered ledges. To the south it was clear with only isolated thunderstorms along the 60 miles to Santa Fe.

We fooled Leonard Crow Dog and turned south over the Navajo Trail as fast as our compass could swing. No Sioux medicine man would be called upon to bring rain in Navajo country, I assured the nervous passengers.

Sliding down the valley I checked the clock, remembering that the Navajo do not honor daylight savings time. Only the White Man, according to the Navajo, would be crazy enough to think humans can fool the sun.

A relief stop in Santa Fe meant decision time again. The airplane was running perfectly. Texas was just around the mountain and we had two good hours of daylight left.

Forecasts, however, were not good. We would head for Texas, but if we could not get past the thunderstorm line, we'd turn back and let Leonard Crow Dog win.

Ah, wide open spaces!

No more mountains—just miles and miles of flat ranchland with nary a tree in sight. East of Bovina the evidence that Crow Dog had already been this way was clear. Below us the land was flooded by the downpours he'd prayed upon the fields.

Near Lubbock we caught up with the night and the clouds.

This time we filed for instrument flight and climbed over them.

Nighttime above the clouds is a delicious feeling. Even when you've been cramped in and out of an airplane since sun-up. We were past Spur when the clouds opened beneath us, and the lights of Aspermont, Jayton and Rule blinked us easily toward Haskell Municipal.

Leonard Crow Dog had already come and gone.

Our five-hour trip had turned into 14. With the 206 snug in the hangar I reflected on the flying lessons I had learned years ago that once again proved true:

Always have a plan.

Always have plenty of options.

Always have patience.

Above all, when things go wrong always go back to the basics. Hold heading, hold altitude and hold on to good judgment. An oil leak and a bad magneto plus unreliable weather in unfamiliar territory present solvable problems, not desperation situations if you heed the above.

To treat them otherwise is to become a needless fatality.

One more thing:

Try to stay on the good side of Leonard Crow Dog. You never know when you may need a Sioux medicine man.

*He whiled the months away until there was enough...for a wingless 1947
Cessna 140.*

14

Making the Magic

Can these bones live? —Ezekiel 37:3

———————

At one time or another, all writers are thieves.

When a word, phrase, tone, shape or style of writing moves us, we quietly "borrow" it for our own.

Most of the time we do it unconsciously.

Sometimes we do it deliberately.

"Making the Magic" is really writer Rick Smith's story about an old guitar player. I stole it back in 1979 to tell my story of an old duster pilot. For years I lived with the guilt and then finally confessed to Rick what I had done.

He confessed to me he had probably stolen the story from someone else, but he couldn't remember who.

Both of our stories are absolutely true. Both really happened the way we wrote them...at least to us they did.

Centuries ago Demetrius said, "Every one reveals his own soul in his letters." If you are a good writer, the real person behind the words shows through no matter how hard you try to disguise yourself behind the print on the paper.

So be careful what you steal. You may find yourself believing it really happened that way...and it probably did.

———————

When I bought a 1947 Cessna (22nd hand) a few months ago I noticed a worn groove, about finger width, on the side of the once-plastic-now-wooden knob on the throttle.

The woman who offered the airplane in a *Trade-a-Plane* ad apologized for the defect.

"The airplane belongs to my father. He used to sit in it a lot and just push the throttle in and out. I guess he wore that place out rubbing his finger on the wood when he played like he was flying."

Her father had been an early day barnstormer-duster pilot, she said.

Flying old elephant-ear Travelaire 4000s he had toured the oily boom towns of West Texas, plunking down in fields and on country roads after drawing a crowd by rocking his wings as he buzzed the square.

You wouldn't recognize his name, and neither did I.

He was just a cowboy turned aviator, flying for chicken fries and enough gas money to take an old biplane a little farther west.

Barnstorming and crop dusting weren't good livings and many times ends didn't come close to meeting.

When that happened he would drop out of the flying circuit for a few weeks and work at odd jobs: fixing flats, sweeping floors, digging postholes.

But always, soon as he could afford to, he'd buy another junky old airplane, patch it up with some "dope" (liquid paste varnish) and Grade A cotton, buzz another square, dust another patch.

Back in the air again.

He was good, she said, a dandy pilot.

Under his stumpy, brown fingers the old round engine crooned to life, purring across Texas prairies and fields. On dead calm mornings his spreader fogged a perfect swath down the rows.

Off-season he'd wow the crowds doing acrobatics. Pulling straight up into a hammerhead, then plunging straight down into a grass-clipping pull-out.

He was good.

But so were a thousand others just like him in a hundred other towns doing the same tricks for the same crowds on the same sunny days.

A few, she allowed, might even have been better.

That handful went on to the airlines.

The rest stayed in Texas.

He stayed.

Stayed and fell in love with a girl he met while working a town in the Panhandle.

Stayed and settled down. Sold his airplane for rent money and went on to other work. Other jobs.

Another life.

He never got rich, the reformed barnstormer-duster pilot. He never even did well. But he raised a family in time and retired at 65 just like his friends.

At 85, wife dead, living with a married daughter near Stephen-ville, a strange thing happened.

He got the itch to fly again.

Once more he wanted to make the engine roar so loud and so smooth that little boys stood wide-eyed and little girls squealed as it swooped over dusty red turnrows.

He wanted his magic back again.

He needed an airplane.

Saving his little Social Security checks he whiled the months away until there was enough. Enough for a wingless 1947 Cessna 140 fuselage that would fit under the old wash shed out behind the house.

Alone at last with his dreams and his airplane he got down to business. He tightened the engine mounts, polished what was left of the fuselage, cleaned the spark plugs. Ready to make the magic roar come pounding into his ears again.

But it didn't.

What came out when he pushed the starter and moved the throttle forward were rough, sputtering gasps.

He couldn't make the magic happen.

There were gaps in his memory where carburetors and wiring diagrams used to be. The little engine died every time he got it going because the touch just wasn't there anymore.

But he tried. Oh, how he tried.

For weeks, for months.

Looking for the magic. Looking for what he had known so well for so long.

But nothing ever worked.

After hours of pitiful fumbling every day he would settle back into the seat and just gently push and pull the throttle in and out, in and out, in and out, gripping the wooden knob someone had stuck on the throttle rod when the plastic one broke. And he'd cry like a duster pilot with his eyes burning from sulphur. Cry like a lonely old man whose last dream just died.

His daughter finally sold the airplane, not out of spite but out of kindness, out of love.

Out of sight, out of mind. It seemed to help.

He died about a year later, and with him his magic.

I think about him once in awhile. I think about him whenever I look at that wingless little 140 sitting in my hangar about to be rebuilt by younger men who will have no trouble making the engine run smoothly.

Making the magic.

I feel the even notch his finger wore in the wooden knob when I sit in the seat—worn while he remembered flying old, forgotten fields.

I can never know the old man's magic. But I feel its presence just the same.

A friend of mine who sat in my airplane once said he could fill the ugly notch with putty and make the knob as good as new.

I thanked him, but said no.

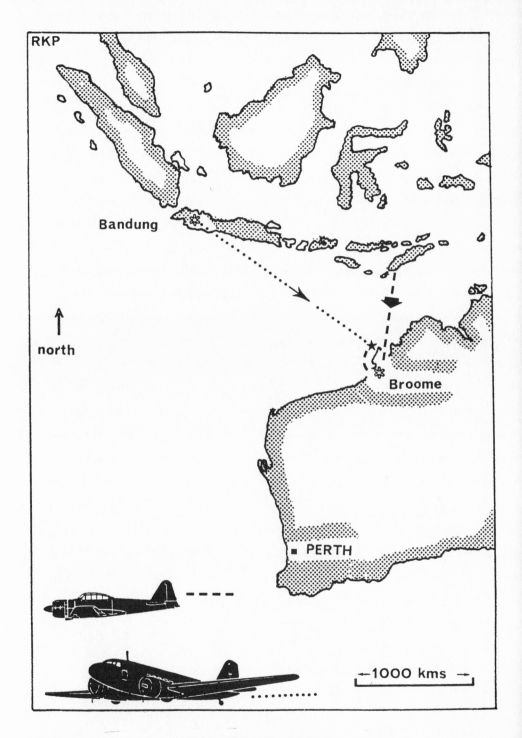

RKP

Bandung

north

Broome

PERTH

←1000 kms→

Courtesy Robert Kendall Piper

Explorer

You must search
Other lands
For hidden treasure?

Then go.
But know

I will laugh
When you learn
Another
Has found
Riches
You never
Read.

Has tasted
Words.
Lines and
Spaces...
Discovered
Hidden places
Searching *me,*
Instead.

15

Last Flight of the Diamond Dakota

For where your treasure is, there will your heart be also. —Matthew 6:21

By night on my bed it haunts me. . . I can keep it to myself no longer. You must be told.

There is a strange sort of madness that comes over those who traverse the nighttime skies of far West Texas. Something about the state's vast darkness that unlocks the secret thoughts of the soul.

It was on just such an occasion that I found myself flying with a grizzled old charter pilot who smelled of oil and stale coffee. He'd not said much—we were nearly over Marathon when he remarked in a barely audible tone about the similarities between West Texas terrain and that of Western Australia.

He had spent some time there, he said, flying cargo and passengers between Broome and Perth.

"I'll go back someday. . ." he stopped himself short.

Perhaps it was the way he gripped the yoke, then fidgeted with the mixture control that told me there was more.

Indeed, there was.

Now you must promise me if you decide to pursue this, all will be at your own risk. You'll not hold me responsible for the talk of a charter pilot in the midnight hour over Marathon.

We are agreed?

Good.

I will now relate to you his account of the last flight of the *Diamond Dakota*.

If you travel west of West Texas you will eventually arrive on the island of Java. It was at Bandung where Captain Ivan Smirnoff in the year of 1942 was about to depart. A minute before Captain Smirnoff was to start engines, the airfield manager opened the cabin door of his DC3 transport and thrust a sealed cigar-box sized container into his hands.

"Take good care of this. It is quite valuable," he gasped before scurrying back down out of the Douglas.

What the Russian-born Dutch pilot did not realize then was that he had been made responsible for more than $12 million of precious diamonds, and that their final whereabouts would spark controversy that still flares today.

Night after night in early 1942 Captain Smirnoff had been plodding his Douglas transport back and forth over lonely seas between Java and Australia. The flights involved evacuating Royal Netherlands Indies Airlines personnel, civilians and servicemen due to the reports of a coming Japanese invasion. There was no assistance with radio or weather forecasts. As the Japanese advance drew closer and closer the withdrawal grew correspondingly more desperate.

The "Turc" (as his close friends called him) anticipated that each trip might be his last. On the night of March 3, it was.

At 1:00 a.m. just as the engines were being started, Captain Smirnoff had been handed the box, wrapped in brown paper and covered with a multitude of seals.

"It will be collected at the other end by an Australian bank," he was told.

Captain Smirnoff, annoyed at being delayed by what seemed such a trivial matter, tossed the container into the aircraft's strongbox and taxied out. The camouflaged DC3 lined up into the wind and roared down the strip into the night. On board was Smirnoff's crew and nine passengers, including one woman with an 18-month-old baby.

Just after sunrise the aircraft approached Broome, Australia. Captain Smirnoff and his co-pilot began to sense something amiss while still more than 100 miles north of the town. Huge billowing clouds of black smoke were erupting into the sky. They had unwittingly stumbled straight into the aftermath of Broome's first devastating air raid by the Japanese. Three "Zeros" led by Lieutenant Zenziro Miyano flew at the Dutch transport, and in their first passes from the port side their fire wounded Captain Smirnoff several times in both his arms and hip.

Despite shock and loss of blood, the World-War I veteran pilot hung grimly to the controls and threw the DC3 into a steep spiral dive. Several passengers, including the woman, were hit by Zero fire. When the port engine burst into flames, Captain Smirnoff elected for a hasty beach landing. As the Douglas rolled to a stop he skillfully swung the nose into the edge of the surf, effectively dousing the engine fire. The crew and passengers evacuated the plane, reasoning that safer shelter could be found in the water under the Douglas.

Waves were pounding the aircraft fuselage, and as a passenger stepped out of the door one of these bowled him down. The wooden box he had been instructed to carry was knocked from his grasp and disappeared into the foam. Given the situation, and as its contents were unknown, no special search was made for it.

It was four days later that a rescue party from a German mission at Beagle Bay arrived after being told of the crash site by a passing Aborigine. Unfortunately, it was too late for several of the passengers, including the woman and baby.

Sometime after his recovery, Captain Smirnoff had a surprise visit from an official of the Commonwealth Bank and a detective. They demanded in no uncertain terms to be told exactly where the brown-paper package was. Only then did the surprised "Turc" learn what the contents were: a king's ransom in diamonds.

Meanwhile, well-known Broome beachcomber Jack Palmer sailed into the area where the *Dakota* had crashed. True to the nature of his profession he went to the DC3 and salvaged what items could be collected quickly. Sometime during this venture at low tide, he chanced upon the mystery box. The fortune that appeared in front of his eyes when he broke it open must have been like a beachcomber's mirage come true:

A sparkling collection of diamonds and not an owner in sight!

The old charter pilot says that from this point on it is difficult to sort fact from fiction. Palmer is said to have paid a visit to Army headquarters at Broome sometime later asking to sign up for service. While discussing the matter with the commanding officer he unexpectedly poured a salt shaker full of diamonds over the officer's desk. The stones were promptly confiscated and Palmer was taken into custody. Later, he was acquitted of theft charges.

Diamonds began popping up everywhere: among Aborigines, with a Chinese trader. . . buried in petrol cans. Some were found after the war in the fork of a tree. Stones eventually accounted for by the authorities totaled "a mere $2 million."

"You mean there are still $10 million in diamonds missing?" I asked.

"To this day—never recovered," my pilot whispered with a shake of his head and another adjustment to the mixture control.

Should you be fortunate enough to visit the land of kangaroos and koalas, you'll find the wreckage of the *Diamond Dakota* has disappeared from Broome's beach.

Ivan Smirnoff is dead.

So is Jack Palmer.

But the diamonds are still there.

And men like those old charter pilots who follow the trails of the nighttime West Texas sky dream of finding them...

Someday.

If my grandfather had had just one of those metal birds we would all be living in tepees instead of houses. (Bill Masters refueling WWII TBM owned by Tommy Wofford.)

16

Independence Day

They made us many promises, more than I can remember. But they only kept one: They promised to take our land. . . and they took it. —Chief Red Cloud of the Oglala Sioux

---

The Indian Calendar

The Moon of
  Frost on the Tepee (January)
  The Dark Red Calves (February)
  The Snowblind (March)
  The Red Grass Appearing (April)
  The Shedding Ponies (May)
  Making Fat (June)
  Ripe Cherries (July)
  The Scarlet Plums (Early September)
  The Black Calf (Late September)
  The Changing Season (October)
  The Falling Leaves (November)
  The Popping Trees (December)

President Andrew Johnson unknowingly may have done more to solve the conflicts between the Indians and the destitute southern refugees pouring into Texas after the Civil War than all the peace treaties ever written on paper.

Johnson sent 47-year-old General William Tecumseh Sherman, perhaps the most hated name in southern vocabulary at that time, to assist the government's Peace Commission, which was to arrange for "negotiating the resettlement" of all Indians from western lands the United States government now wanted to take.

Between Sherman and success stood the Sioux. The name Sioux comes from an old Chippewa word meaning "enemy" or "adder."

The Kiowa Indians, who primarily ranged south of the Arkansas River, were part of the Athapaskan family. The Kiowa were not closely allied with the Sioux, but neither were they like the Pawnee, whom the Sioux utterly despised. To be a friend of the Pawnee was to be a dead man to the Sioux.

When word reached Texas of Sherman's new position as military chief on the Plains, there was instant outrage. The smoke of Sherman's fires was still a stench in every Confederate's nostrils.

Although Sherman may have had some understanding of the Indians' plight as evidenced in his early negotiations with the Navajo, his later words sent back to the Great Father in Washington spoke louder to the Kiowa than his actions:

"The more Indians we can kill this year, the less will have to be killed the next war."

Sherman's words were swiftly carried on the wind by the intricate communication system of the Indians that needed no wire. The Kiowa announced they would join with their Sioux brothers against the Bluecoated Great Warrior with the Evil Coyote Spirit.

A nest of die-hard Confederate rebels rode into Texas in 1868 to try to salvage what was left of their lives.

When a small band of renegade Kiowa en route to join the Sioux against Sherman accidentally rode into this camp of bedraggled settlers on Turkey Creek in the Moon of the Falling

Leaves (November), they were just as unhappy to be eyeball to eyeball with the *Wasichus* as the Rebels were to be within arrow distance of the Kiowa.

Suddenly, one of the Indians pointed forward and shouted in broken, but clear, English: "Death-Sherman-all-Bluecoats!"

The startled Rebels, believing there must be Union soldiers behind them, abruptly turned from their position facing the Indians and began charging the creek where they assumed Sherman and his soldiers must be hiding.

The surprised Kiowa realized the only thing that could make the Gray-Clads angry enough to ignore *them* had to be the presence of their *most*-hated enemy, the Great Warrior Sherman.

Kiowa and Confederate alike swept across the creekbank, each hoping to be the one to find the man who epitomized the cause of their miseries.

When it became obvious no one was present except Kiowa and Confederates, a stocky red-head named Graham called to the disappointed troops to head back to their camp. The equally disappointed Kiowa followed at a careful distance.

By now the huge kettle of coffee left boiling on the campfire filled the frosty morning air with an irresistible aroma. With some hesitation Graham motioned to the cautious Kiowa to join the group.

The Indians eased forward just long enough to take a cup of the steaming liquid, which Graham sprinkled with sugar and crumbled bits of leftover biscuits, then retreated to where their horses were tied to sit on the ground and happily slurp the thickened concoction.

There was no conversation.

None was needed.

Cups empty, the Kiowa silently mounted and rode away.

I was always fascinated by a yellowed piece of cross-stitch that hung behind a cracked glass in a wooden oval frame on the wall above Mama Rob's bed.

"He who hates my enemy is my friend," it said.

It was made by Mama Rob's mother, Callie McQueen Graham, in 1891...

The year William Tecumseh Sherman died.

The Fourth of July has never been quite the same to me since I met Charlie Two Toes.

It was three years ago at the annual Independence Day Fly-in Breakfast at the Colorado City, Texas, Municipal Airport. Charlie was squatted against the hangar, eyes like two brown trickles in a wrinkled, weathered face that had seen 79 other Independence Days.

"Nobody can remember his real name," the lady serving coffee in the breakfast line told me when she saw me staring at the wadded human hunkered alone under the American flag hanging limp in the sultry morning stillness.

"Somebody nicknamed him 'Charlie Two Toes' when he was a kid and I guess it just stuck."

Charlie wasn't eating breakfast. He came only to watch the people line up along the tarmac for the best bacon and eggs and grilled toast to be found this side of the Rio Grande.

Colorado City might be one of a hundred little Texas towns along West Interstate 20, but it has carved out a name for itself around the country with its Fourth of July Fly-in.

Nothing fancy. Just good food, fine hospitality and fun for anyone who enjoys seeing an assortment of airplanes gather at a remote air strip that was once used for military jet training.

But it's more than that. Breakfast in the hangar at Colorado City on the Fourth of July is a sacred pilgrimage. It is a tradition I cling to in order to keep perspective in a world too rapidly changing.

In addition to the assortment of airplanes, there was also an assortment of people continually shifting position to take advantage of the smatterings of shade. Maybe that's what caught my attention about Charlie. The sinewy old man was stationary, moving only his eyes as an airplane arrived or departed.

Or it might have been his pipe. Unlike Charlie, it was shiny new.

I got an extra cup of coffee and wandered toward him.

"What do you think about all these airplanes, Charlie?"

Seeing him up close he looked awfully thin. Ground up into powder he wouldn't make a bullet.

"I think if my grandfather had had just *one* of those metal birds we would all be living in tepees instead of houses today," he said flatly.

He spoke so articulately I jumped. Charlie touched his pipe and smiled. It always startled people when they heard him speak perfectly good English.

His grandfather was Lone Wolf, the famous Kiowa Chief, he said. Back in the great days of the Kiowa rule, Lone Wolf used the high plateau to the northeast of Colorado City as a lookout.

That was before the *Wasichus*—the White Men—came.

After the Wasichus arrived, Lone Wolf in desperation joined with eight other Indian chiefs to save their tribes from annihilation by signing the Treaty of Medicine Lodge in which the Kiowa agreed for the first time to be placed on a reservation.

I wanted to offer Charlie a ride in my airplane, but I wondered how I would get his gnarled legs untangled from their squat and into the back seat of the BT-13. Instead, I crouched beside him, bracing my shoes like he braced his bare feet in the dirt and matching his lean against the hangar.

When I asked if he had ever been for an airplane ride he stared me straight in the eye.

"Sure. Every year. Independence Day."

The way he said "Independence" made it hard for me to swallow my coffee. He tapped his pipe gently on the hangar wall and turned his look past me toward the sky.

"Girl like you don't know a lot about independence. No one does until they lose it."

He tapped the pipe again.

"Do you know why the Indians lost their independence?"

He didn't wait for me to answer.

"Because the Wasichus got theirs."

He drew a coyote in the dirt with his finger.

"I was born where there weren't any walls. A couple of years ago I decided I didn't want to die inside walls. So I went back to the blanket. . ."

He grinned.

"The government told me they would give me a house. Everybody thought I was crazy when I told them I didn't want it because it was square. When they put my grandfathers in square boxes to live they lost their power."

He erased the coyote with his tobacco-stained fingers.

My legs were numb from the knees down. I tried to wiggle my toes but my shoes held them tightly in place. Charlie noticed my squirming and shook his head in amusement.

"Don't misunderstand, Girl. I am not trying to right the wrongs of history. I am just worried. Real worried."

We had to wait for a twin turboprop to shut down before I could ask him what he was worried about.

"You," he said with a touch of sarcasm disguised in kindness.

"You and all these nice people out here celebrating Independence Day. Flying airplanes. Eating breakfast. Waving flags.

"When they put my grandfather on the reservation the first thing they took away from him was his horse. Then his weapons. Then his pipe.

"Someday the government will do the same to you. You pilots are just like my grandfather and the old chiefs who took their freedoms for granted. You think they will last forever, like Lone Wolf thought the buffalo would last forever."

He smoked silently while I sweltered in the heat. It wasn't just the sun that made my face hot. Charlie had me pegged and he knew it. Me and every other citizen celebrating Independence Day.

The pilot of a Cherokee called for Charlie to climb in for a ride and the scrawny Indian was gone before I could blink.

I hurried to take his picture—an old warrior ready to mount 160 horses.

Charlie refused.

"Girl, it will shorten my life if you take away my shadow."

He climbed into the right seat and they were gone in a puff of dust with Charlie waving to everyone like a kid riding a merry-go-round pony.

Each year at the Fly-in Breakfast in Colorado City I ask about Charlie Two Toes. I'm told he is still around, but he doesn't make it out to the Independence Day celebration any more.

I sit by the hangar where he used to sit. The same place where a hundred and fifty years ago it was buffalo, not Bonanzas, raising clouds of dust on the horizon.

I watch people flying their airplanes loaded with all the equipment the government now requires. I watch them eating at tables with "no smoking" signs on them.

I listen to them talk about independence as if it will last forever.

And sometimes I worry. I really worry.

Companion

I sat in darkness and waited.
And when you did not come I cried.
And when I could cry no more I left.
But Darkness...
              Went with me.

17

Black Duster

And the Lord said unto Moses, Stretch out thine hand toward heaven, that there may be darkness over the land. . . even darkness which may be felt. —Exodus 10

It was the perfect night for a Christmas party.

At least, it seemed that way when the familiar "thunk" of the wheels retracting and the "gear up" amber light after takeoff told us we were only 20 minutes away from our Fisher County Airport destination.

A gentle climb to 4,500 gave plenty of time to enjoy the Christmas lights below. Outlines of rooftops and driveways and trees shimmering in red and green gave the whole landscape spreading beneath us the look of hard sugar ribbon candy.

Santa would have no trouble finding me with only five more nights to go before Christmas Eve (assuming, of course, he didn't know about all those naughties when I should have been nice).

Now Santa will tell you that things can change rapidly in West Texas when it comes to the weather, and the Monday night before Christmas was no exception. Sixteen miles northwest of Abilene a line that had appeared to be only a distant shadow on the horizon began to loom dark before us.

It wasn't in the forecast. It wasn't visible on the radar. It just hung there in still silence like a theater curtain waiting for the next performance.

I knew immediately what it was.

You don't live in West Texas all of your life without knowing a "Black Duster" when you see one.

A Black Duster is a dust storm at night. Instead of blowing through in gusty swirls like daytime dust storms, it patiently suffocates, quietly strangling every trace of light and breath before you even know it is upon you.

I experienced my first Black Duster on Christmas Eve 1955. I had been selected to play the part of the angel in the church Christmas program who brought the shepherds the news of Jesus' birth. It was the most coveted of all parts with the exception of the role of Mary, which was given to Billie Sue Koonce. She was a year older than me and too tall to stand on the top step of the baptistery without having her face hidden by the velvet valance.

For weeks I practiced climbing up and down the steps of the baptistery wearing a sparkling white robe made from one of Mama's old sheets and a halo-crown made of glitter and pipe cleaners.

Then came the night of the Christmas program.

I had just made my appearance and delivered those immortal words—"Fear not, for behold I bring you good tidings of great joy"—when suddenly the town tornado siren drowned out the shepherds' singing about the little town of Bethlehem.

The singing stopped and the shepherds, with me in the lead, went every direction.

I stumbled down the steps and headed out the back door, only to find the parking lot swallowed up in Black Duster darkness. Back inside the church Mama kept playing the piano while Brother Red urged everyone to sit down because surely there had been some mistake.

It was too late.

Mary, Joseph, the Wise Men and Herod had all followed me out the door. Every kid in West Texas knew when the tornado siren blew you ran for the cellar, Christmas program or not.

Well, they rounded us all up coughing and wheezing and herded us back into the church. Mama gave me her sternest you're-going-to-be-sorry look, while Brother Red assured us it was just dust in the circuit that had set off the tornado warning.

We started again. One of the shepherds had lost his shepherd's staff cane and a Wise Man had ripped a big tear down the back of his royal bathrobe.

My once-white angel's robe looked like someone had used it to shine boots.

My pipe cleaner halo crown was nowhere to be found.

You never forget a Black Duster. No way. Not even 30 years later when you're flying a fine airplane with the best of technology.

We did a one-eighty and then circled to the north. We were exactly on course with Fisher County Airport six miles ahead when the dust began to thin.

Nobody at the Christmas party believed me when I told them we'd just flown through a Black Duster. I guess they don't believe in Santa Claus, either.

By the time we left Fisher County Airport, the Black Duster had silently moved on east. The wheels had barely thunked in the gear wells when we could see Elmdale and beyond. As bright as it was when we'd left four hours earlier, it was even brighter in the midnight hour.

Ah, Lord. Thank you for light. Thank you for *The Light* in a world often unaware of how dark darkness can be.

Nancy Robinson could not read or write.

18

Mail Haul

The following is a true account of today's airmail and its pilots. The names of the pilot and his company have been changed to protect my innocence.

"Remember, boys, nothing on God's earth must stop the United States mail." —John Butterfield, 1857.

A piece of loose tin rattles eerily in the wind.

The vacant rows of buildings which only a few days ago were hangars full of airplanes are now nothing more than empty holes of darkness. In the shadows before sunrise they look naked and ashamed of their desolation as traffic on Highway 277 speeds by.

The sound of my crunching feet moving slowly through the snow stops for a moment. It will be just a matter of time before the noise of banging metal stops, too, as these hangars are to be dismantled to make room for another industry.

Like hundreds of small airports across America, progress got in the way of Butterfield Trail Airport.

Its brief, but busy existence came to the end of the line when the reality of receding economics rendered it extinct.

121

Instead of paving the runway, Butterfield Trail's new owners put in a pipeyard.

According to the National Rural Letter Carriers Association, there are 47,453 rural mail routes in the United States and Puerto Rico. But not for long.

Recently I received notice that due to the technological requirements of the 911 emergency service, I would no longer live on Rural Route 8, but would have a street name and number as my mailing address.

I do not want to be a street name and number.

The fact is a great deal of my education in the facts of life can be attributed to the rural free delivery mail carriers.

Perhaps I had best explain.

When Mama canceled her subscription to the "pornographic" hometown newspaper, she failed to take into consideration the fact that we would still read it while visiting my grandmother, whose RFD mail box was located on a post at the corner of the road that turned north of her house.

Dr. Brinkley's rusted lid treatment did not solve Mama Rob's arthritis problem, so if I was in the vicinity when the rural mail carrier passed she would dispatch me to retrieve the mail.

Rural route recipients frequently were on mailing lists that city deliveries were not. By the time I had returned to her kitchen, I had thoroughly perused every pamphlet, catalog and brochure for patent medicine that she routinely received.

Patent-medicine literature, I quickly learned, was very explicit about the most intimate details of human life. The postal service, since the passing of the Pure Food and Drug Act in 1906, had done its best to stop the use of the mails for false advertisements and fraudulent claims of cures for everything from indigestion to infertility. However, they were still not entirely successful by the middle of the century.

We did not get such revealing information in our mailbox at home, which was adjacent to the front door and had been assigned a street address. Or at least if we did, Mama got it first and we never had the vicarious pleasure of learning the variety of uses of Nature's Compound from sworn testimonials of users who did not blush to tell RFD readers about the results.

If it had not been for the rural mail carrier, I would never have heard, much less seen an example of, Granny Gray's Cream Cure for Flat Bosoms ("made with real dairy cow cream") which she addressed to "Female-Only Rural Route Patrons."

Granny assured farm women her product would make it unnecessary for them to buy expensive inflation bras, which "do not fit properly, cost too much money and will not attract any man who has an understanding of the true feminine physique."

I wonder, now that I am on a street address and not a rural route, if I will stop getting the advertisements that come to my mailbox marked "For Females Only."

As pioneer efforts of some considerable magnitude, the disappearance of Butterfield Trail Airport may not compare with the disappearance of rural route addresses.

Both, however, represent another piece of America gone.

————

It is New Year's Eve, one mile above West Texas.

There are no horns, no confetti and no tinkling glasses aboard the twin Comanche. Just its pilot, one passenger and a dozen cloth bags stacked where the rear seats used to be. Sandwiched between the glitter of the stars above and the lights below, the mail plane travels an invisible sky-trail westward.

For the airmail pilot calling a position report over the microphone to a faceless voice at Center, it is just another night's work.

It is barely 11 p.m. Already we have been flying for five hours. Before the last celebrant calls it an evening, our cargo will weigh approximately 700 pounds and represent $30 million.

We are carrying canceled checks—worthless pieces of paper until they reach the clearinghouse in Dallas where the banks they were processed through will be given credit in the nation's Federal Reserve money exchange.

We are not alone in the midnight sky.

We are one of hundreds of general aviation airplanes chartered to transport nightly an average of $4 billion to the offices of the Reserve.

It is essential that these airplanes fly. The sum of all these checks in transit makes up the "float." One of the tasks the Fed has in trying to control the nation's money supply is keeping the size of the "float" as low and stable as possible.

It works like this: A check given to a local grocery store one morning might be deposited that afternoon in a bank where it is processed in the accounting section. By evening it is taken to the airport. The check will then be flown to a clearinghouse where the local bank will be given credit for the amount of the check. Then the check will be put back on the plane and returned to the bank.

All before the night is over.

Tonight, I am flying with Conrad, chief pilot of Mohawk Aviation. Mohawk is a private business that contracts with banks to fly their checks. Though permitted to fly the mail run with him this New Year's Eve, I know that passengers are seldom welcomed.

"A minute lost on the schedule can mean failure. If one of these bags is worth a million dollars and misses its destination deadline by one minute, a day's interest could be lost to the bank that shipped it," he said as he eyed me coldly.

"I tolerate no delays."

Now I know how Waterman L. Ormsby felt.

On New Year's Eve, 1858, Ormsby, a special correspondent for the *New York Herald*, was a passenger on the westbound trip of the Butterfield Stage. Contracted to form an overland mail service via a southern route, John Butterfield's Concord coaches never stopped rumbling across the vast, desolate expanses of rolling plains except to trade mule teams, take on more mail and get food for the travelers.

Ormsby wrote of his New Year's Eve breakfast: "We stopped at the station called Abercrombie Pass [Mountain Pass that is west of Abilene] to get breakfast which consisted of coffee, tough beef and butterless shortcake. The drivers ate without stopping or complaining and I dared not do likewise."

Rummaging through the brown paper sack that contains our breakfast, I try to make as little fuss as possible. We are having baloney and bread.

Things haven't changed much, Mr. Ormsby, when it comes to a mail-hauler's meager menu.

San Angelo, Colorado City, Midland. . . then we head east. The weather is perfect.

Clear.

Sharp.

Visibility unlimited.

Three times we stop along the trail just long enough to take on more checks. Then to Dallas Love Field where ground couriers take our bags of checks and scurry away into the early morning hours while we catch a quick nap at Mohawk's offices. By 4 a.m. we are up and loading the plane with bags that might contain the same checks we brought a few hours ago.

Ormsby described his Concord coach bed as "horribly uncomfortable, but adequate when compared to the ground. Besides, as long as we were moving I felt no fear for the Comanches who I knew to be lurking behind every clump of brush."

On Love Field's runways, plenty of Comanches were lurking, all awaiting clearance to take off into the clouds that had rolled in while we were asleep. Conrad's eyes never leave the gauges as we climb to break out above the overcast.

Sunrise is behind us and Abilene is just waking up to a New Year when our night's work is done.

We are on time and on schedule, and for the first time Conrad smiles. In the harshness of the bright sunlight, his stern expression appears relaxed and tired. Like the Butterfield Trail mail haulers, he is a hero whose name will be remembered by few. He follows in the wingwash of those early heroes who forged an airmail route from Abilene to El Paso and on through Guadalupe Pass.

A memorial was erected on top of the 8,757-foot Guadalupe Peak as a tribute to the airmail pilots who used the peak for navigation.

Clearing the Guadalupe Mountains was a rugged chore, and several airmail pilots lost their lives attempting to maintain John Butterfield's declaration that "nothing must stop the United States mail."

Before leaving the airport, Conrad checks for the evening's forecast.

Tomorrow night while you sleep, he must fly.

19

Crooked Rows

I bet when your Dad flew to heven [sic] *the angels in God's control tower said, "Not bad for a first solo."*
                                        Your frend [sic] *who has never been flying.*
                                                                    Walter

P.S. I know what a solo is because I read a story about Charles Lindbergh. He was neat. You would like him.

I had been dreading the Halloween party at school ever since the teacher had sent us home with notes telling our parents we were to wear our trick-or-treat costumes to school that day.

I did not have a trick-or-treat costume.

Mama read the note and sighed. We were living on borrowed money hoping this would be the year we made a good cotton crop.

It wasn't to be.

By the end of October the gins had already shut down and our "crop" of mostly dry burrs was waiting to be plowed under. This was the seventh year in a row of drought. Where my Daddy got the courage to hang on to his faith and his farm I'll never know.

Mama had an idea. She produced two threadbare brown towels from the bathroom cabinet and instructed Daddy to bring her a sack of what was left of the cotton bolls. Then she spread the towels on the kitchen table and covered them with cotton bolls using my school glue to make them stick.

When the glue dried she sewed the two towels together, leaving a hole just large enough for my head. She slid the "towel toga" over my shoulders and wrapped a piece of brown burlap tow sack around my waist.

"There! You can go to the Halloween party dressed as a bale of cotton!" she exclaimed, beaming with the success of her creativity.

It was the most awful Halloween costume I ever imagined. I had heard Daddy describe an old mossbacked cow as being "ugly enough to make a freight train take a dirt road" and now I knew exactly what he meant.

I told Mama I did not want to be a bale of cotton. I wanted to be a fairy princess like the one advertised in the catalog with a fluffy pink net skirt, a satin top and a sequin-sparkled wand. All for the price of $9.98 (The matching pink ballerina slippers were extra.)

Mama cried when I showed it to her.

"Maybe next year we can order this," she said wiping her eyes.

I was surprised.

I didn't know Mama wanted to be a fairy princess for Halloween, too.

Mama said "maybe next year" so many times I didn't much believe her. But I was a cotton farmer's daughter and I decided if she could wait to be a fairy princess, so could I.

Besides, my scuffed brown oxfords matched those old brown towels perfectly.

I made it to school with only a couple of the glued-on bolls falling off. Mama told me if any of the kids laughed at my costume it would just be because they were jealous. By now I didn't much care. All I wanted to do was get this Halloween party business over with, take my trick-or-treat bag made from one of Daddy's cotton sample sacks and go home. At least I could look forward to the school Thanksgiving party—you didn't have to wear a stupid costume for that.

When I walked into our classroom there were store-bought costumes everywhere, including at least six pink fairy princesses. All were wearing the pink ballerina slippers. There were several pirates and cowboys and Indians and lots of ghosts and goblins...

But I was the only bale of cotton in the bunch.

"Wow, that's a *real* costume," one of the ghosts hollered.

"How did you get that cotton to stay in your hair?" an admiring cowboy quizzed. Mama had glued some bolls on her headscarf and wrapped it around my head.

"I'll trade you my wand for your sack," one of the fairy princesses begged.

"No way," I said, making sure everyone could see the side where "Property of U.S.D.A." was printed in big letters.

When it came time for the kids to vote for the best costume in the class, guess who won by a landslide—or maybe I should say by a turnrow?

As part of my honor I got to lead the Halloween parade down the hall where the whole school could see us in our costumes. By the time the last bell rang every teacher had asked for me to come to her room so her class could get a close look at a "living" bale of cotton.

I ran all the way down our road with my plastic jack-o-lantern prize, cotton bolls dropping behind me and out of breath with excitement to tell Mama I had won First Place. This was the very best Halloween of my whole life!

Just before I got to the house, however, I slowed to a walk.

I was also going to have to tell Mama I didn't want to be a fairy princess for Halloween next year. Even though I knew she had her heart set on us wearing pink ballerina slippers.

———

Daddy died.

Ever since I shared his experience of his first plane ride to M.D. Anderson Hospital in Houston, hardly a week has gone by that someone has not asked me how he is getting along.

Rice farmers from Arkansas, cattle ranchers from Wyoming and even dairy owners in Australia shared the six-year saga of his ordeal. Each expressed his admiration for a man who was determined to live, no matter how many times he looked Death straight in the eye.

Considering that Daddy stood six-foot-six, Death had to stay on his toes just to keep up with H.D. Robinson.

The day Daddy climbed into the airplane with me to make that first trip to Houston was one of the few times I'd ever seen the man scared. It wasn't the surgery or even the thought of never coming home to the farm again that had him white-knuckled—it was having to ride in an airplane.

He had arms strong enough to split a bale of cotton in one stroke (he was well known across Texas as the best cotton sampler around when men rather than machines cut a portion of each bale to be graded), but even before we left the ground he was shaking so hard he couldn't buckle the seatbelt.

For all of his fear of flying, Daddy did his best to accept having a pilot for a daughter. For a man who had learned farming from walking behind a team and a plow, he was completely liberated in his belief that a piece of machinery did not know whether you were a man or a woman—it only knew whether you operated it correctly. He had indoctrinated my sister and brother and me with that idea from the time we were big enough to ride on the red tractor with him.

Still, when it came to airplanes, he worried. Let one pass overhead and he'd hurry outside to see if it might be me. We had an agreement that I'd "waggle my wings" to let him know. He'd tease me that his crooked rows were caused by his watching the sky expecting to see me come over while he plowed.

After 19 operations, 42 cobalt radiation treatments and years of suffering the most unspeakable acts committed in the name of cancer therapy, it became impossible for him to plow. It was all he could do to make the 40-mile drive three times a week to the nearest kidney dialysis treatment center.

At first I offered to fly him back and forth, but he said nothing doing. He'd manage on his own. His greatest agony wasn't the physical pain. It was the humiliation he experienced as he grew weaker and weaker. Fingers that had once gripped a sampling knife could barely hold a cereal spoon.

He never knew that I followed him home from overhead just to be sure he made it back safely. That would have been the final blow.

Daddy's heroes were Jesus Christ, Matt Dillon and Charlie Brown. No one had to decide on Sunday whether we would be in the field or go to church. To Daddy, not taking us to church would have been the same as not putting food on our table.

He had little use for dress shirts with collars never big enough for him to button, undisciplined children and travel maps. He was perfectly content to stay in Jones County. He'd tell me that he wasn't going anywhere farther than the turnrow until he went to Heaven. Before he sold the farm, I tried to take him up for a look at the land he'd loved for 40 years.

He refused.

"I'll see it from the air when the Lord lets me out of this dirt I'm in. You can have 'em sing 'I'll Fly Away' at my funeral," he teased.

He made one other request. He wanted to be buried close to the farm. That way, he said, he'd be near enough to see how the cotton was doing and to gripe if the new owner let the weeds grow.

I held on hard to those little bits of his old sense of humor. They were all I had left of the daddy I once knew.

Things got really rough toward the end. The more he saw himself growing helpless, the more angry and more bitter he became. He fought being taken to the hospital even when he couldn't breathe and finally couldn't move, so I told him we would just do what it took to stop the pain—no more humiliations, holes or hoses. When he quieted down and we were able to talk, he told me that the red tractor had sure been running good and that the ground had never plowed any better.

I squeezed his fingers. Daddy hadn't been able to ride the red tractor for two years.

We did quite a bit of talking as the night wore on. Secret things, like how proud he was of me when I would come flying over, and how all the girls at the ag office always made such a fuss over him because he was my dad. He even said he'd like to go for an airplane ride if God would just let him feel a little better.

I told him God would take care of it.

He did.

Before the next morning, Daddy's body was empty and the victory had been won. Like Teddy Roosevelt, Death had to catch H. D. Robinson sleeping or else there would have been one heck of a fight.

Just north of the airport where I learned to fly is Spring Creek Cemetery. It is surrounded by beautiful cultivated fields. I am sure the young farmer on the red tractor trying to straighten the crooked rows wonders about the airplane that routinely flies slowly over the old Robinson place, then crosses the cemetery, and waggles its wings.

Daddy doesn't have to wonder if it is me anymore.

Daddy knows.

20

Specialty of the House

I'll never eat 'taters again.—Scarlett O'Hara

Hattie Jackson, the lady who helped look after my great-grand-mother Alice Macon, cooked the best red beans and potatoes I ever ate.

She would put some in a bowl to cool on the table in the kitchen while she fed Great-Grandmother lunch in the front bedroom.

On Saturdays when Mama went to town to buy groceries, I was left with Hattie. I could smell those beans and potatoes cooking all morning while I played in the wash shed.

When I was sure Hattie was in the front bedroom I would slip in the back door and eat the entire bowl of savory vegetables. They were seasoned with something Hattie called her "secret specialty."

When she came back to the kitchen Hattie would look real surprised to see her bowl empty.

"Now where do you think Hattie's beans and 'taters went?" she would ask with mock indignation.

We would look in all the cabinets and under the table and even in the broom closet.

"Those beans and 'taters gonna be in big trouble if Hattie ever finds them."

Then she'd give me a hug and feel of my tummy.

"Why, *there's* my beans and *there's* my 'taters," she would tease, poking me gently between hugs. Then we would both laugh till we had the hiccups.

I finally figured out Hattie was putting that bowl out for me on purpose so we could play our little game.

I never told her I knew, though.

I was afraid she would stop hugging me if I did.

One time I sassed Hattie.

Only one time.

She told me to pick up the clothes pins I had been playing with on the kitchen floor and put them back in the bucket in the wash shed.

I told Hattie I didn't have to.

For a big woman Hattie Jackson could move mighty quick.

"Your mama wouldn't leave you with somebody she didn't trust to make you mind," she said holding me firmly by one arm and soundly planting her huge, bony hand on my hinder part.

I wasted no time putting the clothes pins back as I had been told.

I knew Hattie was right about Mama and minding.

The year I was a junior in high school Mama got real sick and I had to take over the family cooking.

What was that "secret specialty" Hattie put in her beans and potatoes that made them so good, I asked Mama, when my best culinary efforts to imitate Hattie's recipe proved disastrous.

"Southern comfort," Mama said.

Somehow I don't think she was talking about the kind that comes in a bottle.

It was a deal my daddy would have loved.

A son of the south from South Carolina with a Rhett Butler voice and a '70 model Piper Cherokee had need of a Super Cub. Would I be interested in a trade?

I matched his drawl and told him I'd have to have some boot.

He said he'd meet me and the Cub in Pine Bluff, Arkansas, with the Cherokee and the cash.

We agreed to a rendezvous at high noon.

They started building Super Cubs in 1950, offsprings of the original 32,000 Piper Cubs made famous training thousands of World War II pilots. With twice the horsepower and all of the fun, the Super Cub's appeal has increased almost in proportion to its price tag. Before the war you could purchase a new Cub with a 65 hp engine for $1,325. Today's new Super Cub retails for better than $30,000.

Any way you figure, it's going to be five hours from Abilene to Pine Bluff in the Cub with one fuel stop and a large brown bag. In that large brown bag you put munchies. Forget the carrot sticks, granola bars and other nutritious items. Go for the good stuff: chocolate cookies and potato chips.

I don't care how much breakfast you eat, you'll be digging into the brown bag before you get east of Hubbard Lake. There's something about the sun making rainbows through the propeller arc and the oil pressure in the green that triggers your appetite while flying cross country.

Ah yes, the oil pressure.

Unlike past flying adventures involving windshields covered with oil, this one would surely be different. This Super Cub with only 600 hours on the engine and fresh out of annual wouldn't dare break a crankshaft or a prop seal.

Not even over the miles of Arkansas trees turning to orange once you have crossed the Little Missouri River.

Hold course.

Eat a potato chip.

Check your time against the marks on the map.

Eat a potato chip.

And another.

And another.

If you have done your navigation right you'll arrive at Paris' Cox Field in 2 hours 33 minutes with a whole sack of potato chips in reserve. You can only do this if every now and then you reach for a chocolate cookie in the brown bag instead of a chip.

Refuel. Only don't drink much because you've got another 2 hours 20 minutes to go. And nothing can be more uncomfortable than a full bladder over the Arkansas trees at Super Cub cruise speed.

Full power.

Let the tail come up.

Ease back on the stick and hold right rudder.

As soon as you are in level climb across the Red River into Oklahoma, open the fresh bag of potato chips. Munch in sequence to the rpm. By the time you are even with Milwood Reservoir and Hope Airport is in sight, you will be well into a second feeding frenzy.

Stop munching just long enough to recheck your position because from here to Pine Bluff the visual references get fewer and farther between. Once you pass the lumberyards at Gurdon it's just one gorgeous line of trees after another, with a couple of small towns cleared in between.

Halfway between Manning and Carthage it happened. You're not going to believe me, but it's true as I live and breathe. I'd just quaffed off the last crumbs in the last potato chip sack and was figuring I had 50 miles to go without a munch when the windshield of the Super Cub began to cloud with droplets of splattered oil.

A glance at the gauges said the oil pressure was holding and engine temperature was normal.

A glance at the terrain said there was nowhere to go but into the trees if the engine quit. However, Super Cubs were not designed for branch landings.

The more the oil blew back on the windshield from the front cowling, the more I wished I'd never seen a potato chip. Or a chocolate cookie. Especially in an airplane that was now bouncing with the noon heat.

An oil leak over Arkansas timberland in an airplane with a waiting buyer only minutes away was enough to make you queasy. Couple that with four hours of chocolate chip cookies and three bags of potato chips and queasy doesn't begin to say it all.

Pine Bluff was on the horizon. Start a gentle climb for every foot of altitude the Cub can get and hold course. Keep that empty potato chip bag close—it might come in handy at any time. I promised God if He would get me to Pine Bluff, I would never eat 'taters again.

Rolling down the Pine Bluff runway with a rolling stomach was a relief no antacid can spell. The prospective buyer was waiting.

I had wobbly knees and a greasy, chocolate smile.

He had a tool box and a signed cashier's check.

We pull the cowling.

Nothing more than a push-rod housing seal that had decided to let go.

No measurable oil loss. A simple aggravation with a simple fix.

He suggested we close the deal over lunch at the airport restaurant. He said the specialty of the house was his favorite: fried potatoes and chocolate cream pie.

I said I'd be delighted, of course.

I hope God and Scarlett O'Hara understand.

Turn-About

For now
I must drift into obscurity—
Your Geisha
Who must dance when you applaud,
Then wait in silence until you come again.

Someday, Busy Man,
It will be me
Who claps.

21

"Remember Goliad"

Brave men die more than just once. In our minds we have buried these men again and again. . . they are ancestors to all of us. We share a common destiny today as Texans because we are all inheritors of their sacrifice. —From address by John Collins, The Fannin Memorial Monument at Presidio La Bahia, Goliad

Goliad plops like the center of a star in the middle of Highway 183, U.S. 59 and Old Spanish Road 239 in southeast Texas.

From 5,500 feet above the San Antonio River that wrinkles its way to the Gulf of Mexico on a steamy hot September afternoon, Goliad shimmers. At night the star illusion is even more pronounced as traffic along these highways lights the five paved beams of the star dissecting the landscape.

Victoria Regional Airport is 25 miles to the east, San Antonio International a hundred miles to the north. To leave an airplane in Victoria and pick up another in San Antonio means stashing the well-worn sectional charts in your equally well-worn suitcase and unfolding the crisp new road map of Texas that the car rental agency so kindly provides.

While it is true that I have seen a whole lot of Texas between takeoffs and landings, it is also true I've seen a whole lot of Texas between landings and takeoffs. Both have brought their share of adventure and a deeper understanding of what it is that makes me love this place some say the devil chose Hell instead of.

Fat enchiladas and my favorite brother were waiting at Blanca's Cafe in San Antonio. Stay on 59 out of Victoria, turn north at the Dairy Queen in Goliad and be at Blanca's just as the cheese melts on the sizzling plate.

At least, that was the plan.

Like far too many Texans, most of my images of Texas history revolve around the Alamo. Of course I knew Goliad was also important, but beyond the phrase "Remember Goliad" there was little I really knew of the details of what happened there.

> The saddest page of Texas history was enacted here on Palm Sunday, March 27, 1836, when the largest sacrifice of life for Texas Independence was offered in the infamous Goliad Massacre."

Neat black words on slick white paper in a seventh-grade history book and that was all. Those words and my lack of further study had not prepared me for the sight of Presidio La Bahia, the only historic site in the state of Texas that appears as it did in 1836, rising on the left of the highway two miles south of downtown Goliad.

Unmarred by street vendors, high-rise hotels and traffic jams above the banks of the River, Presidio La Bahia is the only fully restored Spanish fort in existence in the United States. It is not a mission like the Alamo. It never was. Presidios were built to advance the European invasion by providing protection for soldiers against any and all who would get in the way.

This is where the Texas Revolution was born.

Fat enchiladas and my favorite brother would have to wait. My hands were sweaty with excitement as I left the highway and drove the narrow road to the top of the hill. Against the rapidly setting Texas sun the place looked deserted except for an older Mexican woman sweeping the steps of the entryway.

"We close in a few minutes," she said. Then she glanced at the suitcase in the back seat. "But I will be here a little while longer if you don't mind being alone inside."

Alone? How can any Texan be alone when you stand inside the Presidio's Quadrangle where the *Comancheria*—the Comanche lords—once came thundering through on their horses demanding tribute from the Spanish Comandantes?

Alone? How can any Texan be alone inside the chapel where 92 Texian patriots gathered on December 20, 1835, to sign their names to the first Declaration of Independence from Mexico?

Alone? One cannot be alone inside the soldiers' quarters Colonel James Walker Fannin, Jr., called "Fort Defiance." Here more than twice as many died for Texas than at the Alamo.

There is no such thing as alone at the Presidio La Bahia in Goliad. A thousand voices speak through these walls.

Some were from Georgia.

Some from Louisiana.

Some from Tennessee.

Others were from New York, Pennsylvania, Vermont, Ohio, Maryland, Illinois, Florida, New Hampshire, New Jersey, Kentucky, Alabama, Missouri and the Carolinas.

There are female voices in the echoes, too, like the whispers of Señora Alvarez, a *soldadera*, or female soldier. It was not uncommon in warfare during this period of history in the Western Hemisphere to see women as an integral part of the army camp.

Señora Alvarez is credited with having directly saved the lives of at least 28 Texas freedom fighters involved in the Goliad campaign.

Hush—what's that?

The creak of a door?

The flick of a candle?

The flap of the very first flag of Texas' independence wearing a severed arm grasping a sword painted blood red upon once-white muslin?

Or is it only the silence that screams from the towering granite monument, which now covers the mass grave of Fannin and 400 fallen heroes who were marched outside the Presidio upon Santa Ana's orders to die?

I cry because there are none to hear but me. How many others like me have remembered the Alamo...and forgotten Goliad?

A mist of rain is falling with the night. The caretaker comes to tell me I must leave.

"You will come back?" she asks, locking the massive wooden doors behind me as I dash for the solitary car in the dark, deserted parking lot.

It is more a statement than a question.

Oh, yes. I will be back.

Once you have been to Goliad, my friends, you will never, never be the same again.

22

Top Hand

It's only scary when you lose control. —Larry Clement, Jr., rodeo bull rider

---

Elmer Kelton says a good cowboy has more use for a lantern than a bedroll, referring to the daylight-till-after-dark hours he keeps.

I've known a fair share of good cowboys and I will have to agree with Elmer. The same can also be said for a good bull hauler.

My daddy was one.

Folks said H.D. Robinson knew bull hauling like Elijah knew chariots and fire. The truth was Daddy wanted to be pulling plows instead of hauling cows but by the summer of '53 the drought had shut down any hope of him making a living from a dry land cotton farm.

Congressman Omar Burleson arranged for trainloads of cattle feed to be railed in to help the ranchers. But the drought was so bad the trains could not come fast enough, so the government and the meat packers made a deal with the ranchers to sell their herds for slaughter before nothing was left but carcasses and bones for the soap factories.

"Cows for which men had paid up to three hundred dollars each would do well to bring one hundred dollars," according to historian/author J'Nell Pate in *Livestock Legacy, The Fort Worth Stockyards, 1887-1987.*

Ebb Macon contracted with the area ranchers to furnish trucks to haul the cattle to the Stockyards. He hired Daddy for $25 a week to be the truck driver.

I had never been farther than the farm when I heard my daddy was going to be making regular trips to Fort Worth.

Fort Worth!

I begged Daddy for days to let me go with him on one of his runs, and finally, much to my mother's horror, he agreed.

We left before dawn. The cowboys on the Bunkley Ranch had managed to stack those bulls in so thick you could not tell where heads quit and tails started.

Now I don't know if you ever rode in a '47 International pulling a 32-foot trailer in the middle of August loaded to the axles with bellowing, bawling bovines who must have sensed this was to be their last trail ride. But you can probably guess what it was like. Keep in mind that back then the highway was barely two-lane between Albany, Breckenridge, Palo Pinto and Weatherford. Forty miles an hour was top speed. Since there was no air conditioning, you just rode with the windows down and let the breeze (and the aroma) blow through.

By the time we arrived at the intersection of Fort Worth's Main and Exchange streets half a day later, I was exhausted. Daddy was so busy dodging the crowds of milling Stockyards people he never noticed I was pale with fright from hearing the creaking trailer and watching the near-stampede condition of the terrified animals behind me, not to mention the bumper to bumper traffic jam of all the other trucks and bull haulers jockeying for position at the pens.

In 1953 1,013,390 head of cattle plus 313,092 calves went through the Fort Worth Stockyards. Add 2,602 horses and mules, 543,317 hogs and 960,290 sheep to make a total of 2,832,691 animals of the four-legged variety trampling through "Hell's Half

Acre" (as the Stockyards area was affectionately known) in one year alone.

We waited through the noon hour for our turn to unload, and my visions of eating lunch in a truck stop dissolved into a warm bottle of root beer and a melted candy bar Daddy had stashed in the glove compartment.

We could not take time to dine, Daddy explained, because he had to get the trailer back so the cowboys could re-load it and he could make another run the next day.

We made it back home just after dark. My bony little legs ached from sitting so long and my eyes hurt from counting the bricks in the highway for Daddy to help him stay awake, but at least it had been quieter without the cows.

Daddy apologized to the nervous cowboys who were waiting with another corral of hamburgers-on-the-hoof. We would have made better time coming home if it had not been for the fact the generator kept going out, leaving us without any lights the last hour of the run, Daddy explained to the foreman.

They each rolled themselves a cigarette and let me lick the thin tissue paper to seal them *only* after Daddy made me promise I would not tell Mama he had let me do it.

I promised.

I also promised myself I would never ride a cattle truck to Fort Worth again.

I have embarrassed myself in airplanes a number of times. One of my worst *faux pas*, however, did not occur in the cockpit.

In 1985 Fort Worth Airlines made an attempt at offering regular scheduled passenger service between Abilene and Fort Worth Meacham Field. I was invited to take a tour of the YS-11 60-passenger airplanes while Tom King, president of the company, gave a spiel about the service the airline intended to provide.

I do not know what came over me.

Suddenly, just as he had us all to push back in our plush, reclining, maroon-upholstered seats, I hollered, "Moo-o-o-o" as loud as I could.

The cabin emptied immediately.

After that Tom never did invite me to fly as his guest on Fort Worth Airlines.

Can't say that I blame him, either.

Unfortunately, Fort Worth Airlines did not last as long as the generator in Ebb's '47 International. I don't know what happened to Tom, but something tells me he did not hang up his goggles and go into the trucking business hauling bulls.

It was obvious that he was a *real* cowboy.

The evidence wasn't so much his wrinkled leather skin, or the permanent squint etched around his watery eyes from too much dust and too much sun. It wasn't that he was the only one boarding Atlantic Southeast Airlines Flight 2422 on an 80-degree day wearing a long-sleeved flannel shirt.

You knew he was a real cowboy by the way he paused before stepping into the plane, touched his well-worn "John-B" hat with an equally well-worn hand and said "Howdy, Miss" to the smiling flight attendant.

The old cowboy eased gingerly into the seat beside me. You could see he was uneasy, so I thought I'd try to help.

"Say, that's a nice buckle you're wearing. How long since you won 'Top Hand'?" I asked, watching him fumble with his seat belt.

He'd lopped off a couple of fingers in some long-ago roundup, getting them caught between the rope and saddle horn while taking up a dally on a half-wild cow.

"Prizes are for rodeo cowboys. I worked for wages," he said sharply. "And I worked for this."

He reached into his pocket for his cigarette makings and rolled one out of habit even though he knew he couldn't light up.

"You ride on these little airplanes much?" he quizzed tensely.

"Much as I can—probably as often as you ride a saddle."

He shook his head and eased back into the seat a little more. Arthritis and oft-broken bones had taken their toll on his back and legs.

"Don't do much saddle riding anymore—too old."

"How old is too old to ride the range?" I asked, expecting him not to answer.

He fooled me.

"Started up on the Pitchfork in '33—I've cowboyed all over, but I ain't never rode a horse like this."

The more he talked the less he fidgeted.

I think it made him feel easier talking to a woman like me.

He adjusted his hat for the umpteenth time, "Never been flying in my life—unless you count all the times some broom-tail horse sent me straight up."

The airplane's engines were turning.

"Reckon those boys know how to get this thing off the ground?"

I assured him the crew in the cockpit were as good a pair of wranglers as you could find in any outfit. He wiped the sweat from his face with a faded red handkerchief and took a couple of deep breaths. You could tell he'd have rather come upon a den of rattlesnakes than been sitting in that seat.

Takeoff was smooth. Solid. Easy. We were climbing through the overcast east of Moran before he spoke again.

"Glad to see it cloudy—hope we get some rain."

He tried to make it sound sincere, but it came out weak as new-boiled coffee. It worries a cowboy when he can't see the ground.

Suddenly the clouds broke beneath us.

"Hey, look at those fences down there. Looks to me like a dry summer—grass already gone.

"Hey...would you look at that! I've worked many an hour on that bunch of blades! Sorriest excuse for a windmill I ever saw...well, there's the old Diller place...one time me and Diller...

"Hey..."

His story was lost in the drone of the propellers.

"Hey, I never thought I'd get to see this country from above till I crossed the Divide..."

The flight attendant poured a Coca-Cola for him. He told her it was a waste without a shot of Jack Daniels. But he took it and drank it in one swallow.

"Been dreadin' this airplane trip for a long time. But, hey, it hasn't turned out to be half bad." He didn't sound nervous anymore.

"Somebody told me it would be noisy flying on a little airplane—hey, they don't know what noise is if they've never listened to a bunch of cows 'beller' all day...

"Hey, a feller could learn to like this flying..."

I asked him why he was going to Dallas.

"Dealin's," he said.

End of conversation.

The airplane settled onto the runway at D/FW with a steady gallop. The old cowboy was sleeping soundly.

"This is a pretty good way for a cowboy to ride the range, wouldn't you say?" I knew he'd need a little time to get woke up before we got off the plane.

He coughed and stirred.

"No complaints. Just wish I'd done it sooner. A man shouldn't wait till he's in my shape to try out a new saddle."

I watched him walk proudly away. Bowed legs and stoved-up limp. A legend in Levis whose name no history book will ever record. Just a Texas cowboy who has seen his share of wind, rain, hail and drought.

Injury, isolation, boredom and loneliness.

Today that didn't matter. Aboard Flight 2422 this cowboy had ridden the wind...

Hey—for 47 minutes he was Top Hand.

23

Voyage to the Bottom of the World: Part One

We've established a region of the world which is totally weapons free and a nuclear free zone. It is a symbol of the ultimate, a beacon shining light of what we can accomplish if we put our minds to it. It would be a shame to bring Antarctica into the realm of world politics. —Captain Brian Shoemaker, Commander, Naval Support Force, Antarctica.

Each of us experiences events in our lives that impact us beyond the immediate moment.

Some are profound.

Others are what I call "pivotal."

We remember the profound, but we usually don't recognize the pivotal even when they are happening.

For example, getting stood up at the altar when I was a blushing beauty of nineteen would qualify as a profound event.

(He was very handsome, very charming and very AWOL from the Army.)

On the other hand, learning to fly airplanes was pivotal.

In the farthest corner of my imagination I never dreamed that by bouncing my way through student pilot touch-and-go's I would one day go and touch the farthest corner of the world.

We were washing the supper dishes when I broke the news to Mama I was going to Antarctica. I would be gone four or five weeks, I said, trying to sound casual over the clatter of pots and pans.

I waited for Mama to tell me how much she would worry about me while I was off on another of my "wild" flying adventures.

This time was different.

"I am not going to worry any more about where you go in those airplanes because God is already there. If He is *there* where you are, why should I worry *here* where you aren't?"

Mama must have made the devil sweat when she said that, because if God had not been in Antarctica, I still would be.

High Noon.

I pretend to be watching the icebergs floating northward some 35,000 feet below the flightdeck of the C-141 Military Airlift Command Starlifter, which is on course due south 1,500 miles off the coast of New Zealand carrying 32,000 pounds of cargo, 60 passengers, a crew of 12 and me.

Secretly, I have not taken my eyes off Al McCrary.

Probably the most experienced pilot in the Military Airlift Command (Reserve), McCrary, as the aircraft commander, will make the decision as to whether or not I reach my ultimate destination on this adventure to end all adventures. I am the newspaper reporter selected this year to travel with MAC "to gather material on missions, crews and aircraft during resupply to New Zealand, Australia and Antarctica."

Decision point is just minutes away and McCrary shows it.

On takeoff we were given weather forecasts of superb conditions for landing on the six-foot thick ice runway on the Ross Ice Shelf at McMurdo Station. Already the ice is getting "crumbly" as it does in the austral summer of Antarctica from September to

February when the sun never sets. We are the next to the last of this year's 20 MAC flights bringing in the most essential of supplies in support of the four United States Antarctica bases and the National Science Foundation. Everything from videotapes of Dallas Cowboy football games to a year's supply of vegetables is in our cargo bay. All supplies for Antarctica must be ordered a year and often two years in advance.

Temperatures that dip as low as 126 degrees below zero make Antarctica the coldest place on earth. It is also the driest and the windiest. In spite of being covered by more than 7 million cubic miles of ice (about 90 percent of the world's fresh water) there is almost no precipitation. Antarctica averages less than two inches of snow each year. Once the snow does fall, it is blown about the surface until the flakes are compressed into more ice.

Although it was forecast to be clear with winds straight down the McMurdo runway at 10 knots, I knew all too well how quickly conditions could change by the time we reached our PSR—Point of Safe Return. That is the place where the aircraft has sufficient fuel to safely return to New Zealand. Once the PSR is passed, you are committed for landing on the ice. There is no turning back and no avoiding what you may encounter ahead.

"We have enough fuel to hold for about four hours," yesterday's aircraft commander, Jim Martin, had told me. "But we have to weigh all the information and be sure it's the right thing before we go in under less than good conditions."

Yesterday was less than good—55 knot winds, totally obscured sky with blowing snow cutting visibility to 300 yards. It was a "condition one" for aircraft and ground crew operations, so we turned back.

It was a good judgment call.

Stories are told among the crews of high winds known as "Herbies" and "White-outs" that make it impossible to judge horizons, distances or even locations. Herbies are created when fierce winds blow snow or ice crystals through the atmosphere obscuring vision. White-outs occur when the sky and the surface assume a uniform blurring—a hand held in front of your face cannot be seen. Katabatic winds from the Polar Plateau often exceed hurricane force and have been recorded in excess of 200 mph.

Twice in the previous week I had loaded my cold weather survival gear consisting of parka, mittens, face mask cap, socks and "mukluks" (enormous lace-up boots imperative for protection of your feet) and boarded the airplane along with scientists from Germany, France and Japan. These scientists and those of all of the 37 nations who have agreed to the Antarctic Treaty ratified in 1961, are working in the most unique spirit of cooperation in the world. This treaty provides for the Antarctic to be an International Continent, with a freezing of all political claims and total freedom in the pursuit of scientific results and the exchange of results.

"We're the only unarmed military task force in the world," Captain Brian Shoemaker explained. "We don't even own a pistol."

Shoemaker, who is commander of the Naval Support Force in Antarctica, is a piercing, articulate man who readily points out the shadow on Antarctica's future horizon: "There are new nations with territorial claims who want to divide the continent. Any of the treaty members may call for a review of the treaty. That's when the whole world is going to know a lot more about Antarctica than they do now."

In the back of the airplane, loadmasters Roger Wilson and Jim Van Curren keep a constant check on the temperature and the condition of the passengers and cargo. Normally, the C-141 doesn't have a navigator, thanks to the wonders of the little black box known as the inertial navigation system—"INS." But on this run there is one—Chuck Morton, who verifies our heading as we sight the Bellany Islands south of Tasmania. Relief pilot Mike Tracey snoozes in the upper bunk. Flight engineers Don Kurtz and Bill Johns plot our fuel consumption, and in the left seat pilot

Eddie Stokes reviews the approach charts for his first landing on the ice.

I watch Al McCrary.

If we don't make it today, I will have to forfeit forever my chance to make footprints on a frozen continent. My orders call for me to depart for Australia on Monday where MAC will be just as busy hauling supplies to the Outback. . . A MAC Mission Observer isn't there just to see the sights—she is there to see what really goes on in the day-to-day grind of what sometimes can be an unglamorous and thankless job.

A female voice calls out to us from McMurdo radio:
"2031 you are fading out. Change to frequency. . ."
The transmission is lost. McCrary calls again and again before we finally receive the latest weather briefing update. From his expression I can tell little. Stokes also listens and watches.
Suddenly McCrary grins and points his left hand forward.

We are "go" for the ice!

I thought I heard the whine of Scott's long-dead huskies in the wind.

24

Voyage to the Bottom of the World: Part Two

It will happen to you, Nancy. It's called the gee-whiz-look-at-that stage. It's something everyone who goes to Antarctica experiences. For some it lasts a few weeks or months. . . and some just never get over it.
—Walt Seelig, New Zealand National Science Foundation representative.

My stomach hurt.

I'd flown 12,000 miles, survived survival training, learned how to do everything from mushing dogs to breathing without freezing my lungs, and now I was within 40 minutes of what was either going to be the greatest thrill or the biggest disappointment of a lifetime.

"Antarctica is the kind of challenging assignment people compete for," Major John Beattie, commander of Detachment 2, 619th Military Airlift Support Squadron at Christchurch, New Zealand, had told me over and over during my final week in preparation before today's mission. His eyes would twinkle knowingly when I shook my head in disbelief.

Ah, Beattie! You and Seelig and all the others who have seen what I am now seeing—you were right!

155

The reason my stomach hurt was from my seatbelt cutting against it as I strained as hard as I could to see every inch of the spectacle that was spreading before me and the other MAC crew members on the flight deck of the C-141 Starlifter. Our visual target was a 10,000- by 300-foot runway, which the day before had been erased by one of Antarctica's unrestrained snowstorms. Navy crews had worked around the clock to get it cleared for our arrival. Antarctica is "ship duty" for those who serve at McMurdo Base.

This year's weather is on record as being the absolute worst summer in the history of MAC support flights to the "land of fire and ice at the bottom of the world," as the continent was first described by early explorers in the 19th century. The ice was evident, but why the fire?

The answer loomed before us. Sixty miles from the ice runway at McMurdo Station, the active volcano Mount Erebus spewed smoke and steam from its red lava crater as a welcome to the goggle-eyed visitors. Ross Island, situated on the edge of the permanent Ross Ice Shelf in McMurdo Sound is, in fact, a volcanic island of lava poured from now-extinct Mount Terror and Mount Bird, and the still active Mount Erebus.

Walt Seelig had me pegged correctly. I would be one of those who would never get over it.

In spite of the staggering vision of steam and ashes rising into the freezing deep blue Antarctic sky ahead of us, the crew of the C-141 was not distracted from the first priority—that of setting the 250,000 pounds of airplane, scientists and supplies precisely on the icy landing strip.

We make a pass overhead to take a look-see, then fall behind an LC-130 ski-equipped Navy transport on final. There are six of these ski-equipped aircraft in service across the continent. They go where larger aircraft cannot go, working in areas so small and so remote there may be only two or three people based there. In addition to the ski-130s, helicoptors also are flown by the Navy in Antarctica.

"We're the only nation that can go anywhere in Antarctica," Naval Support Commander Brian Shoemaker had told me earlier. "We're there protecting our interests and the interests of science—to maintain presence, if you please. And the other countries better well understand it."

Shoemaker likes to be specific.

Gear down, pilot Stokes watches the ski-130 slide onto the ice. Since 1970 the Air Force has pursued a "Total Force" policy. Highly proficient personnel like Stokes, who is a civilian airline flight engineer and a member of the Air Force Reserves, are incorporated into the day-to-day operations to improve our overall ability to get the most done for our defense dollar. In the weeks I traveled with MAC, I saw absolutely no difference in quality, capability or commitment between active duty and reserve personnel.

In the right seat, aircraft commander Al McCrary coaches Stokes through his first Antarctic approach—McCrary has done it more than a dozen times before. To land on the ice you must be "ice-qualified." To become ice-qualified, you must make your first landing under the supervision of an ice-qualified instructor.

There is a delay.

The ski-130 cannot get off the slick runway quickly.

Stokes pushes the throttles up and executes a missed approach. We circle back and try again, with the wind perfectly calm and visibility so clear you can see the Transantarctic Mountains as if they were only a skip across the ice. For all its wild beauty, distance deception can be deadly in Antarctica.

Then, just like they wrote it in the textbook, Stokes makes a perfect landing. Mount Erebus shoots a fresh puff of steam and smoking ice to welcome us.

The first woman came to Antarctica in 1969. One of our passengers on today's flight is marine biologist Lin Craft, a charming and talented lady whose specialty is diving under the ice for study and photography. Lin will be spending the next five weeks in pursuit of the mysteries of science that are bringing Antarctica into the world's focus. Two countries, Argentina and Chile, began family colonization of Antarctica, bringing the first patter of little feet to the ice in 1977.

Will these children soon claim the continent as theirs by birthright?

The stinging cold makes me squeal as I clump across the glaze in an intoxicating moment. . . I've made it to the uttermost part of the earth. The crew laughs when I tell them the only thing Antarctica needs is a few mesquite trees.

Crammed inside the jolting snowcat transport vehicle, we bounce along at minus 30 degrees. A stiff breeze is beginning to blow, dropping temperatures even further. I am reminded not to leave my skin unprotected for any reason because frostbite can occur in a matter of minutes.

While we are taken to headquarters for a briefing and tour of the facilities, our aircraft is being unloaded and refueled for the return trip—a monumental testimony to dedication by the ground crews who work against nature to keep hydraulic lines and systems from freezing and breaking. Part of our crew stays with the airplane, expecting us to return within a few hours.

Their wait will be much longer than planned.

A myriad of power lines, pipes and buildings where a thousand people are living and working this summer surround the room where we wait. Nearby New Zealand Scott Base is clearly visible—come the winter darkness, only 80 or 90 people will remain to winter over. As intriguing as it may be, I don't want to be one of them.

"We have a problem," Captain Shoemaker slowly announces to those of us waiting to begin our tour. "We have a possible case of cholera at Scott Base—you may be quarantined here unless I can be sure you haven't been exposed."

Cholera! Visions flash through my mind of Christmas in West Texas—without me. Shoemaker is reassuring. "We really don't believe it is cholera, but we can't take any chances."

We are told we can continue our tour while we await the quarantine verdict, but we cannot have food until tests prove neither we nor the vegetables we brought in carry one of the world's most dreaded diseases. We make plans to visit Robert Scott's hut, built in 1901 on Hut Point at McMurdo where the explorer began his quest for the South Pole some 750 miles away. Scott was bitterly disappointed after ten years of efforts, to be beaten in his quest by the Norwegian Roald Amundsen, who with four companions, became the first to reach the South Pole in 1911.

It was not until 1928 that the first aircraft, piloted by Carl Eielson, flew over the Antarctic continent. Richard Byrd made the first flight over the South Pole in 1929.

Tramping up the camp trail with the crew of men who might be my last human contact, I thought I heard the whine of Scott's long-dead huskies in the wind. . .

When, I wondered with a shiver, would I leave Antarctica... If at all?

25

Voyage to the Bottom of the World: Part Three

I was involved for all too short a while in an endeavor of peace; an endeavor which taxed my ability as strenuously as any combat.
—Antarctic LC-130 Pilot Marion E. Morris/Operation Deep Freeze

I started to giggle.

Then the giggle turned to laughter, shrieking through the crystal pure air of Antarctica's icy landscape. I was the last in line behind the other aircrew members who were making their way up the trail to the hut of explorer Robert Falcon Scott.

It wasn't the dizzying excitement of leaving my footprints on Antarctica's eternal snows that had me laughing—it was the irony of our situation. We'd just spent the past week trying to get to Antarctica with our load of scientists and supplies and now that we were here, we wondered if we would ever be able to leave! Quarantined without food until it was certain we had not been exposed to a possible case of cholera in the camp, we began to sense the passion that had possessed men like Scott to survive in this environment.

In 1900 the Royal Geographical Society of London appointed the young Royal Navy lieutenant, then 32, as commander of a South Polar expedition. The Ross Sea sector of Antarctica was chosen as the area most suitable for basing the expedition. Scott and his party sailed for the continent in December 1901. They decided to winter over in the shelter of this small rocky promontory now known as Hut Point on the west side of Ross Island. No one could have ever guessed that this was later to become the site of the largest community on the continent, the U.S. McMurdo Naval Station.

Scott actually became the first man to fly over Antarctica when he surveyed the Ross Ice Shelf from a small army balloon in 1902.

During the summer of 1902-03, Scott and two companions set off to the south with the objective of getting as far as possible, perhaps to the Pole itself, which we now know to be some 750 miles away. Bad weather, sick and dying sled dogs, a shortage of food and more particularly a lack of vitamin C, which caused the men to suffer from scurvy, called a halt less than halfway there.

Scott's obsession with Antarctica resulted in the formation of a New British Antarctic Expedition in 1909. The expedition left New Zealand on November 29, 1910, with the news that a Norwegian, Captain Roald Amundsen, was also making final preparations for an assault on the Pole.

I stomped the snow from my mukluks before I stepped inside the cabin—my feet were cold, but dry. It was the Norwegians who discovered that placing long fibered hay with moisture-absorbing properties in boots would prevent socks from freezing to the soles of the feet.

Inside the hut, things appear to be just as they were when Scott's party launched on its grueling journey. Scott experimented with importing Manchurian ponies to Antarctica to replace the husky dogs of early years because he said the employment of dogs on such a drive required a "ruthlessness" he did not possess.

Scott's last ill-fated expedition began early in November 1911. From the onset, it was plagued by misfortune. Two motor cars, considered by many to be the modern replacement for dogs and ponies, were expected to be able to help lay supplies along the route. They proved to be unreliable and failed completely. Scott's ponies sickened rapidly and the last five had to be destroyed.

The dogs fared better, but were turned back to McMurdo when Scott and his party decided to man-haul on to the Pole. They reached the Pole on January 17, 1912—only to find a tent left by Amundsen who had been there one month before. Disheartened and almost completely exhausted, the five set off for the return walk.

All died before reaching camp.

In Scott's hut the meat still hangs in the smoke-room, preserved by dehydration in Antarctica's climate of cold and almost no humidity. Scorched walls from the whale-blubber stove smell as if they were singed only yesterday.

We all fell silent. Unspoken was the thought in each of our minds of what could have been if Scott had had only one of the LC-130 aircraft that routinely fly to the South Pole station in less than three hours.

Antarctic Development Squadron VI accurately bills itself as the world's southernmost airline. Flying ski-equipped 130s for heavy cargo and the UH-11N "Huey" helicopter, the squadron claims one of the highest of safety records. When you consider the conditions and tasks these aircraft and personnel must deal with on a daily basis, such a safety record speaks volumes—especially to pilots like me, who cringe at a stiff crosswind.

The success of Amundsen rested on his excellent planning and his wise employment of dogs rather than ponies, cars or man-hauling as Scott had done. Although a pony may be able to pull the equivalent of 18 dogs, eating only one third as much food as 18 dogs, the cold, hard fact, according to Antarctic journalist John McPherson, "is that dogs may eat dogs, but ponies eat only hay."

Still no word on the cholera situation.

The day blazed into night, though the sun never moved from its position. I was restless with hunger and silent with fear.

I was the only human on the continent who had not had a cholera vaccination.

Loadmasters Wilson and Van Curen had stripped the airplane's cargo bay to have it ready for pallets to be loaded as soon as we were back at Christchurch—another mission had to be flown to the ice before the MAC crew could complete its annual resupply schedule.

I lost track of time.
Of days.
Of when I last bathed.

I was sleeping fitfully dreaming of plowed fields and forgotten lovers when word came telling us we were finally cleared to leave.

We would be carrying sixty passengers with us. Scientists and support personnel who had wintered over during the previous long months of dark isolation.

In record time the airplane was readied by the crew. Most of the passengers shouted as they climbed on board—we were their winged ark in a winter wilderness.

"When you stand and watch the last plane leave for the season before the sun disappears, it is a feeling of isolation you can't describe," one researcher working on seal studies told me. His family would be waiting in Christchurch, he added. "We're going to have Christmas as soon as I get home!"

I did not want family.
I did not want Christmas.
I wanted *food*.

We shared the snacks we had stashed away on the airplane—the aircrew and I—and I thought again of how MAC folks had always looked after me, even when it meant sharing their last candy bar.

The ice takeoff was as exciting as the landing. We were light enough to get off on our first run, climbing out over Mount

Erebus as it smoked its volcanic breath in quick belches. In the distance, someone spotted the penguin rookeries, now carefully protected from man's intrusion.

But how much longer it will be this way is anyone's guess.

As the continent once known as Gondwanaland fell away in the midnight sun behind us, I began to pack away my parka and think about Australia, tomorrow's destination.

It was impossible.

Visions of life at its hardest lived by pioneers on a frozen frontier kept me awake long after others slept. Our presence in Antarctica and the mission I had helped accomplish represents the ultimate in what America's defense efforts are reaching for—brains, not bullets, working together for peace.

You only get two showers a week in Antarctica, but I never felt cleaner in my life.

Texas Gold. *Bronze by T. D. Kelsey, Fort Worth Stockyards*

26

Unassigned Lands

Once we passed Doan's Store on the Red River we were in Oklahoma Territory. We knew we could encounter surprises at any turn. —Doss Robinson, trail driver, 1875

They were called "Pretty Women."

Two hundred years ago the Cherokee Indians established a sacred sorority within their tribe for women who bravely joined in fighting the enemy. The name, Pretty Women, was given as a testimony to their faithfulness, their ability to communicate using only signs and silence, and their trustworthy performance of duties in spite of distractions.

Noted Indian authority Carolyn Niethammer explains that the Pretty Women joined the men at war councils and were expected to advise the war chief on such matters as strategy and time of attack.

They could be young or old.

They could be as ruthless as they could be charming.

In all circumstances the Pretty Woman were those who could be assigned a mission and be depended upon not to get sidetracked until it was completed.

I might have qualified as a Pretty Woman had it not been for a Cherokee airplane, and a surprise encounter with Guthrie, Oklahoma.

The Cherokee climbed smoothly at 85 mph over Interstate 20 like it had done a hundred times before.

Boost pump off.

Check the gauges.

Look around for traffic. Blend left rudder and aileron in the turn.

Let the nose down a little for a good look around.

Roll out on 30 degrees.

"Abilene Departure, Cherokee 6139T departing Elmdale on course Oklahoma City."

Guthrie Municipal Airport lies 28 miles due north of Oklahoma City. At 7,500 feet there was a chance for good tailwinds. If things went as planned, the Cherokee and I would pick up our parts and be back home before evening headwinds could slow us down.

But things don't always go as planned.

In the west a dark gray haze sulked. By the time we'd crossed Red River it was snarling. We held course until Guthrie was in sight, the wind screaming against the airplane like a thousand horses and a thousand riders stampeding through the Oklahoma skies.

The Cherokee was suddenly very uncooperative. It bucked and jerked and argued with the Guthrie Municipal asphalt in a language known only to flying machines with minds of their own.

Wings at last securely lashed to the tie-downs, it was obvious: the Cherokee and I would not see Texas again today.

Now I've always considered people who complained because a flight was canceled on account of bad weather as being downright stupid. People who get upset at the temporary inconvenience of not getting killed in a thunderstorm don't have both their magneto switches on.

This time I complained.

Guthrie, Oklahoma, was not where I wanted to be stranded. For all I knew, Guthrie was just another small town in Oklahoma where nothing ever happened and if it did nobody cared. I borrowed a car with the idea of heading for Oklahoma City.

I never made it. A wrong turn took me to downtown Guthrie—and back a hundred years.

In early March 1889, Congress passed a hasty amendment to the Indian Appropriations Bill that threw some of the last free acres of western land open to claim and settlement. Grover Cleveland signed it, and later the new president, Benjamin Harrison, issued a proclamation setting April 22 as opening date.

Tens of thousands of land hungry citizens gathered at the rim of the Unassigned Lands, which were surrounded by the Indian Territories of the Five Civilized Tribes: the Choctaw, the Chickasaw, the Seminole, the Creek and the Cherokee.

Within six months, brick and sandstone were mortared into exquisite Victorian architecture making Guthrie the showplace of the Territories.

In 1890 Guthrie was Territorial Capital. In 1907, State Capital. In 1910, as a result of political intrigue and amid accusations and gunfire, the Capital was moved to Oklahoma City.

Through the years there were booms and busts, but never enough to destroy the history standing in Guthrie streets. Sixty-five years after the loss of the Capital there was born in Guthrie the largest restored commercial historic district on the largest tract of land listed in the National Register of Historic Places.

Brick streets, underground tunnels connecting the banks with the saloons where gold flowed faster than whiskey, and the world's largest Scottish Rite Masonic Temple all blend together perfectly in Guthrie today.

More than 100 Victorian business buildings of unique design line 15 blocks, and almost 2,300 homes in the town are certified

Victorian. Spend the night in one of the bed and breakfast inns above the saloons on Harrison Street and it's likely you'll sleep where many a young cowboy or dude from the East shared the pleasures of sin with a lady of the evening.

Except for taking time last April to re-enact the Run of '89 when a thousand horses and a thousand riders rode through, the streets are seldom crowded. Hitching posts and Mercedes sit comfortably side by side.

However, a bilingual sign in a store reminds that much has not changed in Guthrie in a hundred years: it is written in English *and* Cherokee. I blush remembering how close I came to missing this detour when the clerk in the store thanks me for including Guthrie in my flight plan.

Morning at Crabtree Aviation is bustling with a dozen pro-pellers turning and yesterday's stranded visitors anxious to be on their way.

Forecast clear and a million, the Cherokee airplane and its pilot head south. Two plus 55 later we're home.

Only one small problem: I forgot the parts.

I'll be happy to make another trip to Guthrie, I assure the disgruntled mechanic.

More than happy.

The vast emptiness of far south Texas

Forked Tongue

You said I was beautiful.
I saw me in your eyes...
And I believed you.

You said I was brilliant.
I saw me in your mind...
And I believed you.

Now you say nothing.
I cannot see me in your silence...

And I believe you.

27

St. Elmo's Fire

Scientists see it as a corona discharge from a trailing edge and talk about electron avalanches, D2 ions and photo emissions. But we know it's really a sign of St. Elmo's divine protection. —*Professional Pilot Magazine*

Antarctica is a long, long way from West Texas.

To get there from here you must travel miles and miles of empty sky over miles and miles of empty ocean. As far as the eye or even the imagination can see, there is only the airplane suspended between the two—one tiny speck in the infinity we call time.

I told you about the adventure to end all adventures when I returned from Antarctica.

But I didn't tell you everything.

I will confess now what I could not then.

There is a stretch between the tiny island of Pago Pago and Sydney, Australia, where you feel you aren't moving at all. In the darkness of night, the endless nothing can evoke every subconscious dread you are able to suppress in daylight.

Was I feeling all right, the Starlifter's weary pilot wanted to know? He was from Georgia and was the nearest thing to Texas

I'd seen in days. How he could see the sickness in my eyes in the dim light of the cockpit I do not know, so I lied and told him I was fine. Just fine.

In truth I was desperately ill, but not with anything a pill could cure.

I was scared.

What, you say? You? Scared?

Yes I was.

Scared sick.

Scared we would never fly out of that endless nothing. Scared I might never see Texas again.

I told him I had never been so far from home in my whole life. He said he understood. That he'd had some of those same feelings many times, but this would be the last. He would be through with flying when this trip was over. He was retiring, going home to Georgia to grow vegetables and never see oceans again.

He motioned me to his left.

What I needed, he told me matter-of-factly holding my hand, was a little dose of St. Elmo's fire.

"Watch," he said. "It always happens right about here." Almost immediately the airplane's windshield beside me began to dance with blue lightning.

For those of you who may not have seen it, St. Elmo's fire is a continuous bluish electrical discharge resembling the limbs of a tree or bush that appears on the outside surface of a windshield in flight. It also can create a bluish glow around propeller tips, refueling probes and other sharp airframe points.

Most easily seen at night, it looks like a miniature lightning display, though the only sound may be the crackling of static in the headset. Depending on atmospheric conditions, it may last for just a few seconds or many minutes. Some encounters have lasted as long as thirty minutes.

According to David Webster, writing in *Professional Pilot* magazine, this phenomenon is a sign of divine protection.

Webster says an ancient sailor of the Mediterranean named it for St. Erasmus, who was martyred during the persecution of Christians under the Roman emperor at the start of the fourth century A.D.

Erasmus was also known as St. Elmo. Legend says he was killed by having his intestines pulled out by a windlass. Perhaps by association with a ship's windlass he became known as the patron saint of sailors. The bluish glow seen on masts of ships in a storm was thought to be a sign of his protection.

Another version of the story says the name originated with a Dominican preacher in Spain who spent much of his time with the sailors and fishermen of the coast.

Regardless of which saint was the inspiration for the name, it has stuck with us from the Old World sailing ships to today's high tech aircraft, which try to slough it off with static wicks, grounding wires and shielded antennas. We also give it less romantic names such as "corona discharge" or "brush discharge," all referring to something still not entirely understood.

Professor Larry Radke, an atmospheric scientist at the University of Washington, says the two types of Saint Elmo's fire, the glowing type and the brush type, are probably the result of two different processes.

"The glowing fire, or corona discharge, can result from being in the presence of a high electrical field such as between the earth and a highly charged cloud."

Radke makes it sound so clinical. Like the school nurse explaining the facts of life in girls' gym class.

"The brush type seen on an aircraft windshield probably occurs when a static electric charge builds up as a result of friction with ice crystals in the air."

I watched the light spitting down the airplane's nose. St. Elmo's fire has been known to enter the cockpit and even roll down the aisle in a ball and exit out the tail.

Suddenly, the light was gone, the airplane's nose swallowed again by the dark.

"You'll be O.K., Nancy. You'll forget all about being homesick when this leg is over," his steady voice drawled. "You'll see Texas again as sure as I'll see Georgia."

Then he squeezed my hand.

Lord, I wanted to tell him I loved him, but I hardly knew his name. We said good-bye later in Sydney and he promised to send me some squash from his first crop if I would promise to remember him every time I saw St. Elmo's fire.

I promised.

It happened again last week just like it has every November since I made footprints on the ice in Antarctica. The fire, that is. Only this time I was flying over the vast emptiness of far south Texas instead of the South Pacific. St. Elmo came skipping across the airplane's windshield and then he was gone.

I explained to those startled passengers flying with me it was nothing more than electron avalanches, D2 ions and photo emissions, a sure sign of divine protection.

Then I asked them if they liked fresh squash.

The girl in my memory I had never really left behind.

Everything an Indian does is in a circle, and that is because the Power of the World always works in circles. —Black Elk of the Oglala Sioux

Poem for the Wa-si-chu (White Man)

You came to me
Opening my hidden doors,
    Feeling where I touch.

I came to you
Brushing against your walls,
    Touching where you feel.

East to East,
West to West.
    Our circles moved apart.

Left behind
Particle of time. . .
    Circle within my heart.

28

The Girl I Left Behind Me

'HO 'ZHO GO CH'AA N'DAA KAI DOO —Navajo's way of saying
Travel with Beauty

There would be no moon tonight.

At 8,500 feet crossing the Sangre de Cristo Mountains of
northern New Mexico, four riders and their winged steed raced
the darkness for Santa Fe's Municipal Airport. We were just
behind the sun—incurable wanderlusts in search of a part of my
past I'd left behind 15 years ago.

I wanted to find *me* again...the footloose-and-fancy-free teen-
ager-just-turned-adult who'd gone to see the world beyond the
Rio Grande for the first time. My only possessions then were a
'65 Chevy, a willowy figure and a fortune in friends. Time has
been kind to me...

I've still got the friends.

I had fallen in love with southern Utah: particularly the can-
yonlands, where water and time have created a stunningly beautiful place known as Bryce Canyon. Bryce Canyon is a fairyland
of carved sandstone pillars undulating for nearly 20 miles in a
series of multicolored spindles and spires. Bryce Canyon has a
magnificence to which the Indians attached spiritual values. And

Ebeneezer Bryce, the first white settler who tried to make a go of
the land in 1875, also gave it a "spiritual" description:
"Well," he said, "it's a hell of a place to lose a cow."

I had never really lost hope of someday going back to this
hallowed sanctuary. Was it the Indian in me or the outlaw? For
it was also here in this remote, once inaccessible place that the
infamous Butch Cassidy began his ride to notoriety.

Born on his father's ranch in Utah, George Leroy Parker grew
up idolizing a cowhand named Mike Cassidy, who taught him to
ride, to shoot and to steal horses and cattle. By the time he was
18, George was helping Cassidy move cattle to Robber's Roost, a
bandit hideout near what is now Bryce Canyon National Park.

He changed his name to Cassidy, joined the McCarty Gang
and on March 30, 1889, with Tom McCarty, he robbed the First
National Bank of Denver of $21,000, making him Utah's most
sought-after outlaw. Later, Butch Cassidy stole the payroll of a
Utah mining camp in broad daylight—a feat that was acclaimed by
other prominent no-goods like Black Jack Ketchum and the
Sundance Kid. They joined together and became branded as "The
Wild Bunch" because of their drinking, carousing and total
unconcern for the law.

Increased pressure from Utah's posses drove Cassidy south,
finally to Bolivia, where he was killed in 1912. "Positively identified," the history books assure us. . . but rumors still thrive in
Utah that Cassidy made it back to Panguitch where he'd last met
his mother at the Blue Pine Hotel.

Like Cassidy, I wanted to make it back to Panguitch one more
time.

We would spend the night in Santa Fe, then strike out across
the land of the Navajo where airstrips bore names like "Chaco
Trading Post" and "Ship Rock." The most magnificent landmark
to westbound pioneers, whether by covered wagon, mule train or

airplane, is the great Ship Rock by the San Juan River, which signals the travelers' entrance into Monument Valley, Arizona.

My fellow air travelers had never been this way before. However, morning over Monument Valley was enough—they, too, began to sense the lure of this country, which is too vast to be perceived from the ground alone. Without the airplane, the overall perspective of 25,000 square miles of enchanted landscape would be lost.

Without the airplane, I would probably never make it back to Bryce Canyon. Years ago when I'd learned to fly, my instructor told me the airplane would not only open the doors to new horizons—it would take me back to old ones as well.

How right he was.

Cliff dwellings, pueblo ruins, hogbacks, mesas, fault lines and hogans passed beneath the shadow of the 210's wings. We took a clearance from Salt Lake Center and climbed to 13,000 feet to get over the mountains when spring clouds made the passes unsafe for visual flight. The time-chiseled sentinels of Monument Valley seemed hauntingly familiar. Perhaps from my childhood love of the celluloid cowboys who either rode into fame and fortune or into the sunset here. The 1938 movie *Stagecoach* introduced the world to Monument Valley, and filmmakers and television producers continue to make it a backdrop for adventure.

We dog-legged it into Cedar City, carefully watching the unpredictable weather this wild country produces at the flick of a Vortac needle. To the west, rain; to the east, a thunderstorm. Ahead, a cold front bumped us in the nose. We'd chosen to land at Cedar City rather than trying our luck on the strip near Bryce Canyon only because no transportation was available at the strip. The 210 could have handled it fine—three passengers, 120 pounds of luggage and a woman in search of her memories.

We were at Sunrise Point in the Canyon before daylight the next morning.

I would tell you what it was like to see Bryce Canyon again, but that is impossible. Fifteen years had passed, yet it was as if nothing had changed at all. The wind still howled, the rocks still glistened, and there I was—a willowy girl again, dancing first on one foot and then the other to keep warm in the mountain morning cold.

Bryce Canyon is ever-changing, and yet unchanged, the travel brochures say.

So is the girl in my memory I had never really left behind at all.

29

Amazing Grace: The Way Willie Sang It

To Whom It May Concern from the Placement Service Office, North Texas State Teachers College
    Reference: Miss LaDelle Macon, B.A. Degree, 1940
    Major: Intermediate Education
    Minors: Music, English
    "Miss Macon is a studious and dependable girl. She is neat and attractive in appearance, full of sparkle and confidence. She has overcome to a remarkable extent the handicap of a meager background. She never complains.
    "Her great improvement may be attributed to her excellent mind and professional zeal. I feel those who get this energetic, warmhearted and intelligent young woman for a teacher may count themselves very lucky indeed." —Mrs. P. Mizell, supervisor, student teaching

---

My sister said Mama must have had one of her bad coughing spells.

My brother said she might have been struck by lightning listening to the radio during the storm.

I said it was typical of Mama to leave us guessing.

The Justice of the Peace declared it a massive heart attack.

183

The police found her sitting in her favorite chair in the living room. She was holding the catalog.

Dead three days.

Mama never did get to order that pair of pink ballerina slippers.

When we got to the funeral home Doris Kinney would not let us see Mama.

"Did the best I could...closed up in the house in this heat...a body bag...remember her the way she was."

Mama had always had this thing about not wanting men to look at her when she was lying down. She even had a double shadow-paneled slip saved back that she had told us to make sure she was wearing under whatever she was buried in.

Doris said the slip wouldn't be necessary, given the circumstances.

We told Doris to put it on her anyway. We knew better than not to mind Mama.

Mama died.

It wasn't supposed to be this way.

She was supposed to have longer than six months to catch up after a lifetime of raising three kids, caring for elderly parents and dutifully waiting on an invalid husband.

Six months and now there's another patch of fresh dirt in the Robinson plot at Spring Creek Cemetery.

Easy to see from the air.

Hard to believe from the heart.

She was enjoying the freedom to stay up all night reading, sleep till noon, eat junk food instead of cooking and listen to country-western music. She knew every song and every singer, which may not seem unusual if you didn't know her.

Few really did.

The worst word I ever heard her say was "shoot." She never wore a pair of jeans (she believed women who wore pants belonged in the field, not in public) and she never drank anything stronger than root beer.

She never flew in an airplane, either.

A lot of folks might have felt sorry for the Robinson kids because we had one of those because-I-said-so mamas.

You know the type: When you ask how come it is you have to go to church on Sunday night while everybody else is going to the movies she said, "because I said so," and that was reason enough.

In spite of the fact we missed out on a few of the "fun" things, we turned out well enough for Mama to be proud.

My sister became a fabulous cook and mother to Mama's only grandchild. My brother earned a master's degree and was the one who followed in Mama's footsteps as a teacher, and, well...two out of three isn't bad.

Mama fell out with me when she heard I was flying airplanes.

Not that she didn't love me, of course. It was just her fear.

It was useless to argue with Mama about how safe flying really is. Or that learning to fly isn't such an unusual thing for a girl to do these days.

I am sure when Mrs. P. Mizell wrote Mama's recommendation and referred to her "professional zeal," she was trying in a nice way to warn folks that Mama had her own opinions. No one but the Lord himself was going to change her mind.

Just between us, He probably gave in and let her have it her way sometimes.

As sure as her gray hair was still naturally curly and her eyesight almost gone, I know that's what He was doing when she left. She was sitting in her favorite chair by the lamp asking God not to let her be a burden one minute, and the next she was skipping down the paths of Glory. An energetic, full of sparkle girl again with eyes that could see the face of Jesus.

Mama was extremely good at keeping secrets. Somehow I'd never thought of her as anything but "Mama" until we were closing down the homeplace and found her old college trunk. Under 50 years of dust we discovered a Mama we didn't know.

A letter earned as a varsity tennis player. . . membership rosters in Drama Club, Camera Club and leading roles in the College Players. There was a transcript of four years of study that proved she had made straight As in physics, chemistry and French. . .

But there weren't any credits for the meals she skipped to buy her books and the hours she cleaned tables in the boarding house to avoid having to ask her parents for more money in order to take extra classes.

There was her letter of application to become the first, second and third-grade teacher "combined" at Girard—the first job she applied for and the first school that hired her. Attached was a picture of a confident, slender girl with laughing eyes we'd never seen before.

She looked just like Mama.

Of course, she always planned to go back to teaching after the babies started. But by the time I showed up she had permanently traded the blackboard for the rub board.

When I began writing an aviation newspaper column, it was for Mama. I knew if I could share my aviation experiences through written words she would understand better why I was a pilot.

It worked. Oh, she never did go for an airplane ride with me. But she became my most avid supporter and my toughest critic.

Not long before she died I told her I was thinking about quitting. Ten years, I said, was long enough to put myself on a piece of paper for people I didn't even know to read me.

"I would be so disappointed," she said in her quiet gentle voice.

It took my flight instructor hours to teach me how to get back on course. Mama did it with just those five words.

She left so suddenly I didn't have time to tell her goodbye.

She wanted it that way. No fuss, no show, no regrets. Some music would be nice, she once told me.

Amazing Grace, the way Willie Nelson sang it.

She never said a word about the time she wowed the entire campus of North Texas State Teachers College with her classical piano recital.

I am sorry now I didn't insist she go flying with me. When I would suggest it she would say she was "too heavy" and tease that the plane might not get off the ground. It was true that she had let herself go physically, but those who listened to her expound on the Scriptures or describe the exact dimensions of the Straits of Hormuz knew she was still that studious and dependable girl with the brilliant mind.

It would be easy to indulge in my grief. Or to be bitter because six months of freedom doesn't seem like a fair shake after all the years Mama spent being responsible for other people's happiness.

She would tell me not to because she is so much better off being with Jesus.

Besides, there are too many stories still to write.

And I don't want to disappoint Mama.

After Landing Checklist

In the days of the old telegrapher's code, "30" meant final.

There are only 29 of my favorite flying stories in this book because I am not finished yet.

Don't worry.

If your favorite is not included, it probably will be in the next collection of 29, which I am already working on.

Someone has said a writer does not die until she uses up all the words she has been allotted.

Ask me what I am going to write about next and I won't be able to tell you.

Ask me which flight was the most exciting, or who was the most interesting person I ever interviewed and I won't be able to tell you.

Then ask me which piece of writing was the most difficult.

Twenty-eight words.

No by-line.

And I had to pay to get it published.

> FOR SALE: PRICELESS OLD FAMILY HOMEPLACE NO LONGER NEEDED BY OWNERS. PERFECT FOR KIDS WHO LOVE SANDPILES, BASEBALL AND SAWHORSES. WELL USED. BARGAIN TO WHOEVER WILL USE WELL.

They don't give a Pulitzer Prize for the best piece of writing in the classified ads section of the newspaper.

Maybe they should.

Daddy doesn't have to wonder if it is me anymore.

To order additional copies of this book

send $21.95 (includes shipping and handling) to:

MasAir Publications
P.O. Box 944
Abilene, TX 79604

Texas residents add $1.37 sales tax